HAUNTED HAPPENINGS

Real Encounters in the UK's Most Haunted Places

WAYNE SPURRIER

DEDICATION

For Hazel, without whom I would never have experienced some of the unexplained moments detailed in this book, nor had the opportunity to explore some of the most amazing and historic locations in the UK.
I am forever grateful for your friendship.

FOREWORD

The idea behind Haunted Happenings came about almost accidentally. I had no aspirations or concept of how the business would evolve, as my fundamental reasoning was purely based on the fascination of ghost hunting and wanting to share this with others. I was not an avid ghost hunter myself but had been lucky enough to experience something paranormal which made me want more. I could never have dreamt how much more though as things very quickly went from strength to strength.

When I started Haunted Happenings I wanted to offer an experience that allowed those taking part to have an authentic investigation. I realised very quickly though that as a business we also had to maintain high standards of ethics and ensure that our guests were always given value for money. We had a strong duty of care to our guests and this had to override everything. With over 50 team members working across the country this is not always easy to do. However, somehow we have not only maintained but increased our quality of experience, and our guests are always assured of a fascinating night of ghost hunting at whatever location they choose to investigate.

Haunted Happenings is the largest and most well-known ghost hunting company of its type, taking literally hundreds of people a week to some amazing locations; it just continues to grow. Ghost Hunting was once an experience that people only watched on TV, but now it is something that is part of many people's weekend activity. In fact, it is so popular that many celebrities are desperate to get involved and test their nerves, as they allow themselves to be taken completely out of their comfort zones.

We have ventured into Europe to ghost hunt at some famous places such as Bran Castle (Dracula's Castle), Hoia Baciu Forest, Ireland and so much more. We have worked with people such as David Hasselhoff, Scott Mills, Cara Delevingne amongst many. Our adventures have been numerous with so many highlights and unforgettable moments along the way.

I could not be more proud of what has been achieved by all those working within Haunted Happenings over the past decade. It has not always been easy and there have been times when it has been all consuming but every time I see the look on a guest's face who is doing this for the first time and has witnessed something paranormal I remember why I began.

I have no idea where Haunted Happenings will go from here, or for how long, but whatever happens it has been an incredible journey shared with incredible people and I am excited to see where our next adventure takes us.

Hopefully we will see you on a ghost hunt very soon.

Hazel

Hazel Ford
Founder and CEO of Haunted Happenings

CHAPTERS

INTRODUCTION

Is there anybody there?

These are quite probably the first tentative words of any ghost hunter's journey into the paranormal. I know they were mine; I remember them vividly. I was standing in a cold, damp cellar. The room was so dark that, regardless of the passing of time, my eyes never adjusted to the blanket of blackness. Even after five minutes had passed I still couldn't see my own hands in front of my face. My heart was thumping so hard in my chest I thought it might burst. My mouth was dry, my hands were sweaty and shaking. I wanted something extraordinary to happen so badly, and yet at the same time I was slightly terrified at what it might be. There was a noise. I froze.

I look back on this moment now, nine years down the line, and smile to myself. I remember those feelings as if they were yesterday. The tension was palpable. The anticipation of what might come was electric. The thrill of the chase was addictive.

Ghost hunting, for me, was nothing short of electrifying, and I was hooked.

But why are so many of us intrigued by stories of ghosts and other-worldly encounters? How can it be that, despite ongoing advances in technology, we have still yet to prove or disprove the existence of ghosts? Nobody can truly answer these questions, but one thing is certain; the popularity of ghost hunting is on the rise, and shows no sign of stopping.

In 2014 an online poll found that 39% of Britons believed a house *can* be haunted. 28% believed they had *felt* the presence of a supernatural being, and even more staggering is that 9% said they *had* communicated with the dead on at least one occasion.

When those percentages are factored into the total population of the country, this poll suggests that around 21 million adults in the UK believe in the afterlife in some way. But maybe the outcome of the poll isn't so surprising after all.

You never have to search for very long before you'll find someone who could talk the hind legs off a donkey on the subject. From first-hand experiences, to stories of their friends' encounters; there's never a shortage of people willing to talk openly and enthusiastically about ghosts.

Although participation in paranormal investigations has grown massively in recent years – predominantly thanks to a number of supernatural-themed television shows – ghost stories have been around for almost as long as man has walked the earth. From Homer to Shakespeare, ghosts have been ever-present in literature throughout the ages, with almost every culture on the planet passing down stories and legends from generation to generation.

Our questions around the existence of ghosts and spirits transcends race, religion and social standing, and the subject is one of the few things which truly unites people with otherwise nothing in common.

Having hosted public events for a number of years with the UK's largest ghost hunting company, one of the things which has struck me is the diversity of those who are fascinated by ghosts; ages spanning from 18 to 80, and from such wide-ranging careers as solicitors and lecturers, to retail assistants and refuse operatives (bin men to you and I).

The desire to know whether there really *is* something waiting for us when we die seems to know no boundaries. But just what is it that excites us so much about the prospect of encountering a ghostly apparition in a haunted house?

Science may have the answer.

When we're scared our bodies release chemicals which, under the right circumstances, can feel good. As human beings we are naturally predisposed with a 'fight or flight' response to potential danger, so when faced with a situation that is controlled (to a certain extent), the adrenaline which courses through the body creates a euphoric feeling.

It's no different to the buzz we get when riding a roller coaster, or facing a bungee jump. Those activities are both controlled environments, yet they contain a level of danger – and this is what creates the thrill. So when faced with entering an allegedly haunted building, where one *may* experience something which takes us outside our comfort zone, the thrill is very similar.

Whatever our beliefs regarding the paranormal, it's the unknown which creates this feeling; the suspense while waiting (and hoping) for something to occur. Sometimes even the bravest or most logically minded people will show signs of fear when exploring such properties, and for that reason ghost hunting – regardless of your beliefs – is a hugely addictive pastime.

The success and enjoyment of a ghost hunt relies heavily upon one factor – trust. We must be able to trust the people involved, and their motives for attending.

Paranormal investigations and public ghost hunting events are, in many ways, very different.

The focus of an investigation is normally scientific in its approach and has one goal; to capture irrefutable evidence that ghosts and spirits are among us. Controlled environments, expensive gadgets, extensive research and a log – to detail dates, times and even temperatures of rooms – are all essential in this situation.

There's no point setting out to capture the audio of a disembodied voice in a crowded room with people talking, or in a space with excessive ambient noise. If you want to convince the world that you have captured something paranormal, you'll need as many supporting elements of proof as possible to substantiate your claim.

But what if you don't want to be the one who proves to the world that ghosts exist? What if you just want to have an experience that is personal to you and gives you the opportunity to challenge or validate your *own* beliefs?

This is where ghost hunting events, organised by companies for regular members of the public to attend, offer the opportunity to do just that.

Since the rise in popularity of *Most Haunted* and *Ghost Adventures* on the television, more and more people have stepped out from the comfort of their armchairs, and into the darkness of the UK's spookiest buildings for themselves; keen to experience the very locations they've seen investigated on TV.

From old Victorian schools and abandoned hospitals, to historic castles and ancient inns, ghost hunting companies across the UK have opened up opportunities for everyday folk to go beyond the threshold, and experience what it's like to take part in a ghost hunt for themselves.

Unlike scientifically driven paranormal investigation teams, these public events don't set out with the intention of capturing and documenting 'evidence' – although there have been many occasions where EVP (electronic voice phenomena) and photographs have revealed stunning results.

Instead, the focus is to offer those with an interest in ghosts to take part in séances and vigils, in an attempt to have their own personal experiences, without judgement or bias towards their beliefs.

It's through these public ghost hunts that I have personally experienced a number of inexplicable events over the past ten years, and it's these stories – along with contributions from other team members – that I would like to share with you in this book.

They come from the personal experiences of a number of genuine ghost hunters. No attempt is made to validate the stories or support them with evidence, and as the reader you don't have to believe a word of that which is written. You make up your own mind!

Take a journey with me into some of the UK's most haunted locations (and one dalliance into eastern-Europe), and immerse yourself in some of the most bizarre experiences from within their walls.

Real places. Real encounters. Real haunted happenings.

1

THE STATION HOTEL
Dudley – West Midlands

The Station Hotel lurks in the shadows of the historic and ominous Dudley Castle, in a region known colloquially as The Black Country.

In recent years it has gained notoriety with ghost enthusiasts for its continued reports of paranormal activity, famously highlighted in 2003 by the television programme *Most Haunted*.

The Black Country encompasses the boroughs of Sandwell, Walsall, Wolverhampton and Dudley, and is an area steeped in Industrial history, where coal mines, brickworks, steel mills and iron foundries once created high levels of air pollution, leading to the inception of its name.

The Station Hotel harbours a long and fascinating history. Once the most prestigious hotel in the area, it boasts an impressive list of famous visitors including Bob Hope, Laurel & Hardy and George Formby. The latter is said to have performed from the balcony of his room to entertain the masses below, following an appearance at the nearby Dudley Hippodrome.

Today the building has lost the glamour of its heyday, although arguably it has retained much of its charm.

The hotel dates back to 1898, with the erection of a black & white Tudor-style building, complete with stables and a courtyard for visitors' carriages. Extensive renovations and modernisations were carried out in the 1930s and 1960s, to satisfy the growing demand driven by the Opera House across the road, and subsequently the Dudley Hippodrome.

Its façade is one of the most recognisable in the area. Tall, slender sash-windows slice into the curves of the dark, red-bricked building, which spans three stories. The hotel's name is emblazoned across the front in gold lettering, and inside, a grand sweeping-staircase leads gracefully from the Victorian style wood-panelled reception desk to the many rooms on the upper floors.

The grandeur of times-gone-by is still evident in tiny nuances throughout the building, but in recent years the hotel has become more widely known for the many reports of ghostly activity encountered within its walls.

There are few surviving records of the earliest history of the Station Hotel, thus making many of the names offered by visiting psychics and mediums difficult to validate, but what cannot be denied is the sheer terror that some of the hotel's guests and staff have endured throughout the years – many of which the hotel team are only too happy to recount.

During the *Most Haunted* investigation, psychic-medium Derek Acorah talked of a well-known folklore, regarding a hotel manager who enticed a young servant girl into the cellar. Legend has it that when she spurned his advances and threatened to reveal the indiscretion to his wife, he murdered her and disposed of her body via the barrel-chute in the bowels of the hotel. Acorah gave the names George and Elizabeth in relation to this story, and asserted that her body remains buried near the front of the property.

Stories of cutlery being disturbed in the dining room are commonplace, and there have been a number of occasions where patrons of the hotel have fled their bedrooms in sheer terror, having experienced inexplicable phenomena.

Room 214 has become synonymous with some of the most frightening encounters at The Station Hotel, with reports of beds moving and shaking while their occupants try to sleep.

Guests have reported waking in the night with such a heavy pressure upon them that they were completely unable to move, and most unnervingly the figure of a woman has allegedly been witnessed sitting in the small chair beside the window of this room.

Who these spirits are, or their purpose for remaining within the hotel's walls, will probably never be known – if they exist at all – but after personally conducting more than twenty ghost hunts at The Station Hotel, I have some of my own stories to tell of this authentic, charming and spooky establishment.

Whispers in the Hallway

On the evening of Saturday 21 September 2013, I had the dubious pleasure of staying the night in room 216, just three doors away from the infamous bedroom in which a number of people have experienced what they believed to be paranormal activity.

The weekend had been an interesting one already, spent in the company of twenty enthusiastic ghost hunters for the first of Haunted Happenings' Dudley Ghost Weekends – two nights spent hunting for paranormal activity at both the hotel and the castle on the hill, with the hotel as our base for the whole weekend.

The event itself had produced some interesting moments, as is often the case here, but it was after the ghost hunt had ended, and everyone had retired to their rooms, that something very strange and unexplained occurred.

I climbed into bed at around 2.25am, and began to make some notes in my mobile phone about the night's experiences, so that I wouldn't forget them by the following day when I'd need to write up a summary for upload to the website.

I'd guess that around five to ten minutes had passed before I became aware of a voice whispering in the corridor, seemingly just outside my door. It was impossible to make out what was being spoken, but it occurred to me this wasn't a conversation. The sounds seemed to be short sentences, followed by spells of silence.

Questions without answers.

I smiled to myself, making the assumption that some of our determined ghost hunters had sneaked back into the hallway to continue their search for activity, especially as this had been the scene of more than one strange incident during the earlier event.

I continued making my notes for around ten minutes, and during this whole time the whispering continued. Always just a few words, followed by silence.

When trying to make communication with the spirit world we naturally ask lots of questions. *Is there anybody there? Can you try to show yourself to me? Are you able to come close to this device I'm holding?*

I often smirk when I imagine people from the past going about their business, wondering why on earth we're so keen to get in their way, bombarding them with one question after another.

This was exactly how the noises from just beyond my doorway sounded. A few words followed by nothing – just emptiness.

Finally, intrigued to find out who had braved the corridor at this unearthly hour, I crept quietly from beneath the warmth of my duvet, slipped on a t-shirt and some jogging bottoms, and ventured towards the door.

Gently gripping the door handle, I quietly unlatched the Yale lock and pulled the door open softly, trying my best not to startle whoever was there, as I didn't want them to jump and wake the whole building with screams of terror.

'It's just me,' I whispered, as I continued widening the gap so I could peek my head around and ask how they were getting on with their solo investigation.

The hallway was empty! A chill spread throughout my spine, tingling one vertebrae after another; a steady frost slowly creeping its way from the base upwards.

Where had they gone?

I knew with absolute certainty that I'd heard the voice just seconds before reaching the door and making my presence known, but now there was nobody to be seen.

The army of people who make up the team for Haunted Happenings are from varying walks of life, have different backgrounds and employments, and have their own stories to tell about what sparked their journey into the search for paranormal activity.

We each have our own views about what constitutes 'paranormal' and yes, there are some who would even still consider themselves fairly sceptical.

This is important though, because without a balanced view and a logical approach to this field, it would be very easy to make assumptions that every tiny noise were a sign from the 'other side'.

From my perspective I can categorically say that, although I have many stories to share about experiences I cannot explain, I am careful to approach each investigation with a clean slate, always seeking obvious explanations before considering that something *could* be paranormal.

Faced with the conflict of what I'd been hearing for the last ten minutes, versus the empty hallway I now looked up and down, I was perplexed and intrigued in equal measure, and set about trying to find the source.

Somebody must have heard me coming and snuck back into their room!

Having taken a moment to click the safety latch onto my door, so I didn't find myself in the embarrassing position of having to visit the reception desk and explain I'd locked myself out of my bedroom, I crept quietly along the whole corridor, listening for a few seconds at each of the rooms, to see if I could hear any movement from within.

One after another I paused, until I'd satisfied myself that all four of the other rooms on this landing were silent – indicating that the occupants were sound asleep.

It occurred to me in the moment that there was no conceivable way anybody could have shifted from the hallway quickly enough to make a hasty exit, as I had kept my approach deliberately silent; the first indication of my presence would have been the sound of my door being unlatched.

I ventured to each end of the dimly-lit corridor, checking as I did for any creaks, to see if it was possible to move along the floor in a hurry without making a noise.

The hallway is carpeted and makes no sound until you reach the two small steps which rise, and separate rooms 213 and 214 from the others. At each end of the corridor there is a heavy fire door, neither of which it is possible to open easily without creating a significant amount of noise.

I knew this already, but to satisfy my inquisitive mind I checked each of them in turn, looking into the stairwells beyond, to ensure nobody was hiding from me.

There was no sign of life, and after listening intently for a few moments in silence, no hint of any sounds I may have misconstrued as a whispering voice.

Never one to miss an opportunity to potentially capture something irrefutably paranormal, I collected my mobile phone from the bedside table and returned to the hallway, switching on the voice recorder as I settled myself.

'If there is somebody here who is trying to speak to me, please try again now,' I asked in a hushed voice.

The silence was deafening.

'If you are here with me now, please tell me your name so I can introduce myself to you properly.'

Still nothing!

A few moments of similar questioning followed before I accepted the inevitable and retired to my bed once more.

I listened intently from the comfort and warmth of my duvet, like a caged animal waiting to spring into action if I heard the voice again, but no further sounds were heard, and I drifted into a deep sleep fairly quickly.

At breakfast the following morning, just a few short hours after the whispering voice had been heard, I questioned every single guest who had been on our event to see if anyone had been back up there or – since the other rooms were being used by our party – if anyone else had heard noises from the hallway after we'd retired to our rooms.

Nobody had anything to report, and all those staying on this corridor that night were couples. As I explained my reasons for asking something dawned upon me.

There was only one voice!

Not only had the whispering appeared to be a series of questions without answers, but there had only been one voice asking them; always the same tone.

Questions without answers. Words, then silence.

Whoever it was I'd heard from my bed in room 216 that night, I now felt certain that none of the ghost hunting guests had been carrying out their own investigation.

The whispering from the hallway will forever remain a mystery to me, but a mystery I would dearly love to experience again, and solve.

Pennies from Heaven

For many ghost hunters and paranormal investigators, much of the thrill comes from the exploration of unusual buildings, or the parts of buildings few people get to see.

Dark corridors with an array of open doorways, spooky architecture which appears to come straight from the reel of a blockbuster horror movie, or places with horrific tales to tell.

At the Station Hotel, it's the cellar space which most are drawn to, and where a great number of people have experienced unusual happenings.

The cellars of the Station Hotel are vast by any building's standards. A network of rooms of varying sizes are accessed by a long tunnel, at the end of which a huge wooden door swings open to reveal yet more corridor, leading to the infamous barrel drop – supposedly the scene of poor Elizabeth's demise at the hands of the wicked hotelier.

The typically Victorian arched ceilings have been whitewashed; peeling, cracked paint further adding to the eerie atmosphere which oozes from the very fabric of the building. A maze of pipes trace the roofline, and when the lights go out you are plunged into absolute blackness.

In the years since the hotel became a haven for paranormal enthusiasts, a number of inexplicable events have been described by those investigating its secrets.

The sounds of keys jangling have been heard on a number of occasions, and people have reported witnessing strange light anomalies throughout this basement area.

On more than one occasion, visiting mediums have sensed that the largest of the rooms was used as a private meeting place for bare-knuckle fighting, with the spirit of an Irish man often being present. Due to the lack of records it's impossible to validate these claims, although these types of gatherings would be unlikely to have been documented anyway, even if the history of the building were better available.

It's within this very room that a truly puzzling experience occurred.

On the evening of Saturday 3 November 2012, a small group of ghost hunters seated themselves around a circular table towards the end of the room. The majority of the group had left the area with our medium, to make a cursory visit to the bedrooms on the second floor, leaving just myself and five guests in the cellars, to begin a short séance.

It was particularly cold that night. Even within the confines of the building, the hazy mist of our breath hung heavily in the air. Everyone was suitably dressed to withstand the freezing temperatures outside, having been instructed to wear layered clothing in preparation for spending time in the draughty cellars.

In the sheer blackness of the room we had planned to call out for the spirits in the hope we could hear or see something, and with such a small group it was easy to ensure we had a controlled environment in which to make our attempts.

'Okay folks,' I began, 'It would be great if you could all place your hands on the table and ensure your little fingers are connected.'

The purpose of this was twofold. Firstly, I intended to request that the spirits make themselves known by trying to use the collective energy of the group, and make a knock on the table that they could all feel. I hoped that by linking everyone together we would be generating maximum energy for the entities to utilise.

In addition, when connecting the group by touch, each and every person would be able to verify – should anyone report hearing or feeling anything – that nobody had moved their hands during the process.

As always I positioned myself several feet away from the group, so there could be no question I'd somehow fabricated anything in the event of us receiving a response.

'Is there anybody in the room with us?' I began. 'If so, could you please make a noise to let us know you're here?'

There was no response.

'Could you try to copy me please?' one of the group asked, before whistling into the darkness.

Again, we received no reply.

The requests continued for several minutes with little success, and it was during these attempts that I decided to try something a little different.

One of the most shocking and alarming paranormal experiences a person can have, is to encounter genuine poltergeist activity.

Across the years there have been a number of highly publicised and well-documented accounts of this phenomena, the two most infamous being those of the Enfield haunting between 1977 and 1979, and the terrifying experiences endured by the Pritchard family at an inconspicuous, semi-detached property on East Drive in Pontefract, North Yorkshire.

The word Poltergeist comes from the German language words *poltern* (to make sound) and *geist* (ghost or spirit); the literal translations therefore being 'loud ghost' or 'noisy spirit'.

In both of the aforementioned cases, the protagonists in the drama were adolescent girls.

It's a common theory among those in the field of psychical research that the energy source for such a haunting is generated by hormonal changes, and the angst often associated with children during puberty.

Either that, or the tension created in an environment by circumstances such as the breakdown of a marriage.

In the case of the Enfield poltergeist both of these boxes were ticked, and some of the activity reported by the family, neighbours and even a serving police officer, is terrifying just to read.

For those who choose to engage in public ghost hunting experiences, or the more evidentially based paranormal investigations, genuine poltergeist activity is one of those phenomena which we seek.

In fact, other than actually seeing a ghost – the Holy Grail for all paranormal enthusiasts – this would be the ultimate display of the paranormal.

'I'm going to throw something,' I announced to the group, wanting to be careful not to startle anyone by making a sudden noise for which they were unprepared.

Reaching into my pocket (still in pitch darkness) I sought out a coin from my loose change, taking care to feel for the sizes to be sure it was small in its value, just in case I couldn't find it afterwards.

The timeframe between announcing my intention and actually throwing the coin could not have been more than one or two seconds. Taking great care to ensure I didn't throw the coin at somebody, I launched it overhead towards the emptiness of the other end of the space.

This particular room is sizeable, possibly around 35ft x 25ft, and we all heard the familiar chink of metal against brickwork as it landed, presumably some 20ft away.

In all honesty I had absolutely no expectation that the coin would be heard to move again, but just as the words began to form on my lips to ask for this to happen, I was stopped in my tracks.

What was that noise?

Standing in the darkness I'd positioned myself around three meters away from the group, who were all seated to my left, with their hands on the table. Yet just a second after hearing the coin land in the distance, a noise came from my right, seemingly close by.

I reached for my torch and clicked the button quickly to investigate the source of the sound. What I saw beside me sent a chill through my whole body.

Beside my right foot, just inches away, was a one penny coin.

I couldn't be certain whether I'd thrown a 1p or 5p into the room, but from its size I knew it had to be one or the other.

I was completely mystified, and instantly began to consider the possibility that one of the group had managed to thrown a second coin in my direction, in an attempt at some elaborate hoax; yet this didn't stack up.

Each and every person in that room was wearing thick winter coats that night, making it impossible to move freely without creating the instantly recognisable sound of fabric brushing together.

There had been no such sound!

Not only that, but since there had been no gap in time between announcing my intention and actually throwing the coin, nobody could possibly have had the opportunity to reach for a penny of their own.

And finally, since I was standing with the group on my left, I would have been blocking the trajectory a coin from their direction would have taken; it would most certainly have hit me instead.

All of these thoughts ran through my mind.

So, having explained my discovery to the group, we set about searching the cellar floor for the other coin; the one I had thrown and we'd all heard land somewhere in the distance just a few moments earlier.

There was no other coin!

Despite a valiant search by the whole group, we simply couldn't find any other coins in the room.

The flooring there is made up of brickwork, with a small gulley running through the centre, measuring approximately 20cm in width.

Logic suggested that perhaps the original coin had somehow hit the kerb at the other end of the room and rolled back, ending its journey with brilliant coincidence right beside the very person who'd thrown it.

Yet, despite several attempts at rolling it from that end of the room, we couldn't even get close to it reaching the same spot. If the brickwork itself didn't stop the coin, then the channel in the floor certainly did.

Besides this, the gap between hearing the coin land (which everyone in the group attested to) and the sound by my side which had alerted me, was less than a second; much quicker than it would have taken for the coin to roll back.

There was one final nail in the coffin of the roll-back theory; there had been no sound.

It would have been impossible for the penny to roll across 20ft of brickwork without making a noise.

Needless to say this experience became a talking point for those in the room, and although I've attempted this several times since that night – in a desperate attempt to find a solution to the riddle of the penny – to this day it remains unsolved.

Did we experience genuine poltergeist activity in the bowels of the Station Hotel? I guess we'll never know for sure, but that's the nature of ghost hunting.

2

DUDLEY CASTLE
Dudley – West Midlands

The skyline of Dudley has been dominated by a castle for over 900 years, the first of which is thought to have been built around the year 1070, shortly after the Norman Conquest.

The original castle was a typical motte & bailey structure; a wooden fortress built atop a raised earthwork mound. However, following the destruction of the original build on the orders of King Henry II, construction began on a stone structure which is thought to have been completed prior to the death of John Somery – the last of the male line of the family dynasty who owned the land – in 1321.

The main gate to the castle and the stone keep we see today – towering over the town below – are both believed to date back to this period of re-building.

Further construction continued well into the 15th century, finally coming to completion in the hands of one of Henry VIII's trusted advisors.

John Dudley was one of England's most powerful and wealthy

men towards the end of the king's reign, and the huge range of buildings added to the castle during this period changed its primary purpose from medieval fortification to palatial residence.

However, the castle was to suffer greatly at the end of the English Civil War, and on 24 July 1750 fire engulfed the structure and raged for more than three days, all but destroying the once splendid property.

If you look closely it is still possible to see streaks of lead on the stonework above the undercroft, a stark reminder of how intensely the great fire had burned.

No attempt was made to re-build the castle following its last misfortune, leading to its demise into the role of a romantic ruin.

As you would expect from a building with such a lengthy and torrid history, there are plenty of ghost stories associated with Dudley Castle and the surrounding grounds.

One such story tells of a woman, believed to be a witch by the community, who lived within the castle grounds. One version of events suggests that she hanged herself from the battlements following the death of her beloved cat, but many believe in a much darker truth; that a group of locals tied a rope around her neck, before throwing her and the cat to their deaths.

During a medieval evening in 1983, the prize for the most authentic costume was apparently awarded to a woman who had arrived dressed in a grey shawl and sackcloth dress. When the organisers came to present the prize she could not be found, yet the officials on the security gate were absolutely certain she had not passed through the gates.

Who was the mysterious woman, and how did she disappear without being seen?

Was she ever really there?

Another well-known ghost of the castle is that of a little drummer boy; killed by a single bullet from a 17th century musket during the English Civil War, while carrying a message between opposing forces. He is said to have been heard on many occasions around the main gate at night, banging his drum as if in battle.

Locals believe that seeing or hearing the little drummer boy is a sign of impending bad luck.

The Grey Lady

Of all the sightings and ghost legends associated with the castle, the most well-known and documented is that of the Grey Lady; thought to be the ghost of a woman by the name of Dorothy Beaumont, who once lived in the castle.

Hers is a story of tragedy, for it's said she suffered the loss of a baby during childbirth; succumbing to death herself a short time later. Her wishes to be buried beside her beloved daughter were not honoured, and it's believed she wanders the grounds of the castle in search of the infant.

A number of sightings and photographs have been documented across the years, believed to be that of the grey lady, and it was during a Sunday morning visit to the castle that I captured one such image myself.

The morning of Sunday 6 June 2010 was warm and sunny. The purpose of the visit was to share in the celebrations of a child's birthday party.

The castle staff had arranged for the children to colour face masks in the undercroft; a notoriously haunted part of the castle in which a stone coffin lies – believed to have once contained the remains of the dastardly John Somery.

While the children enjoyed their activities, completely unaware of the sinister history of their surroundings, a number of photographs were taken to document the day.

Despite having personally experienced several strange incidents in this room during previous ghost hunts, the atmosphere within the undercroft on this morning was nothing but one of happiness and joy, with no hint of anything paranormal; or so it seemed at the time.

Much later in the evening, while sifting through the many images on my camera, something unexpected caught my eye.

In one of the pictures a child can be seen proudly displaying the mask she'd created, but lurking in the background was something altogether more sinister; a figure which most certainly looked out of place.

The birthday party was a private booking and attended by only a handful of adults – all known to each other – along with two members of the castle staff who'd been assigned to entertain the kids. None of the adults were wearing white clothing that day, and the castle team were dressed in their instantly recognisable green fleeces.

But way in the background of the photograph a figure in white can be seen, standing behind the child.

Due to the positioning of a raised platform in that area of the room on the day, it was not possible for a living person to be standing where the figure appeared to be, without themselves being raised by around 1½ feet.

However, a suit of armour positioned on the floor next to the platform offered perspective to the white figure's height, and indicated that the staging would have been cutting right through a person's legs in order to achieve the height and position of the figure. In addition, a bookshelf on the wall appeared to be in front of the figure's shoulder, yet the shelf was fixed to the wall, making this an impossibility too.

Analysis of the photograph, and manipulation of other images taken on the day from roughly the same spot in the undercroft, were inconclusive in finding a logical reason for the shape.

To this day no suitable explanation for the figure in white has been found, yet if you consider the room was filled with the laughter of young children that morning, could this possibly be the manifestation of the grey lady, attracted to the innocence and energy of the children?

After all, if she really does wander the grounds, yearning to be reacquainted with her own child, surely it's plausible to think she would be attracted to the energy of a room full of youthful exuberance?

Mistletoe & Whine

Haunted buildings aren't all about the glamour of the elite. While some of the most powerful figures of English history have walked the now extinct halls of this great castle, one must remember that there would have been an army of 'normal' people working in such a place; those without whom the running of such a grand and palatial property just would not be possible.

Take for example the cooks, serving staff and grounds men. The great and the good aren't the only ones who may still be present in spirit.

When you consider that these people would have massively outnumbered the family themselves, surely a paranormal investigation is more likely to encounter one of these characters, more so than the great figureheads of the time such as John Dudley, or Queen Elizabeth herself.

So it's of little surprise that one of the most seemingly active areas for paranormal happenings across the years, has been in the part of the building which sits beneath the now derelict Sharington Range, where the infamous Duke of Northumberland would have entertained his high and mighty peers during the bloody Tudor era; an 'unseen' part of the castle which would have bustled with workers.

One December night in 2015, during a ghost hunting event, a handful of eager paranormal enthusiasts were to encounter something truly startling in this very area of the castle.

Sometime after midnight, while carrying out a watch and wait vigil in a small room – heavily decorated with Christmas decorations for use as Santa's Grotto – the group seated themselves on the floor and tried to make contact with the spirits of the castle.

In order to rely upon their own senses, rather than some of the paranormal gadgets on offer, they turned out the lights and sat in total blackness, focused completely upon listening for a response to their requests for knocks, or displays of light, as a sign somebody was with them.

A few short minutes into the vigil a rustling noise was heard, and upon investigation with torchlight, a length of tinsel was found to be on the floor in the centre of the room, presumably taken from the Christmas tree which sat in the far corner.

With each of the group seated around the edges of the space, the tinsel was placed upon a small table in the centre – several feet away from anyone's reach.

Due to the extremely cold temperatures that night, everyone in the room was wearing thick winter coats, which made it almost impossible to move without creating noise.

'Can you please do something to let us know you're here?' one of the group requested.

Within moments the sound was heard again, and to everyone's astonishment – when the light was turned back on – the tinsel had once more been thrown to the ground.

Naturally suspicion began to rise within the group; each person strongly believing that one of their own was playing a trick on them by moving the tinsel themselves. But, with everyone positioned several feet from the table, and seated on the floor, this seemed impossible without detection.

The tinsel moved several times during the following fifteen minutes, and each time – as soon as the noise was heard – a torch was switched on, in an attempt to reveal the hoaxer.

Nobody was out of place, and yet the tinsel was always back on the floor.

What the group were totally unaware of at the time, is that several years earlier – in almost exactly the same spot – a torch had been thrown from a table during a similar experiment.

On this occasion the group vigil was being led by one of Haunted Happenings' mediums. A small team of investigators had created a circle around the table, and simply for somewhere easily accessible to put it, the host had placed his torch on a table in the centre of their circle.

Whilst calling out for the spirits of the castle to come forward and make themselves known, a loud bang was heard. Upon inspection it was found that the torch, which had been placed upright onto the table to ensure it didn't roll off, was now on the floor.

Each and every person in that group swore that the hands of the person either side of them had not been released, therefore making it impossible for anyone in the group to have stepped forward and thrown the item to the floor without detection.

Despite several requests to repeat the action no further activity occurred that night, although everyone present was staggered by what they'd seen.

Were these two cases a coincidence, or something more? Did those present experience true poltergeist activity on these nights? It will never be proven either way.

With both incidents taken into account, it would appear that something paranormal – whether sinister or playful – does lurk within the dark recesses of Dudley Castle.

Perhaps one day you will encounter it for yourself.

-3-

WOODCHESTER MANSION
Nympsfield – Gloucestershire

If you were asked to conjure up an image in your mind of a spooky, haunted mansion, you'd probably picture large empty windows, dark passageways and winding staircases; somewhere totally isolated from the outside world and surrounded by woods.

You would probably imagine somewhere very much like Woodchester Mansion – an unfinished Gothic-revival masterpiece, nestled deep within a valley, surrounded by National Trust woodland, and accessed by a mile-long dirt track.

In recent years this gargantuan property has become synonymous with ghostly activity, with many television shows broadcasting paranormal programmes from within its walls. In fact, such is its popularity and reputation with ghost hunting groups, the mansion is rarely overlooked in the lists of most haunted buildings in the UK.

Woodchester Mansion was built sometime around the mid-1850s, on the site of an earlier property called Spring Park.

Constructed largely from local limestone, the building exudes the very essence of Gothic architecture. Stone gargoyles adorn the exterior of the façade, while huge church-like windows stretch skywards, arching into a point at their peak.

However, despite some of the finest craftsmen in the country being commissioned to work on the construction, the building was never completed. In 1868 the workmen downed tools and left Woodchester Mansion, never to return. They are said to have left much of their equipment behind!

It's often speculated that their hasty exit from the job was due to the ghosts which are said to haunt the place, although there are no confirmed records of the departure and therefore this cannot be verified.

In the 1970s it is rumoured that devil worshippers would enter the building after dark to perform satanic rituals in the Chapel area of the property. The land on which Woodchester Mansion is built was never blessed, and a hooded figure has allegedly been witnessed in the corridor around this part of the mansion.

It's possible that the cloaked figure is the ghost of a monk called Brother Michael, who is said to have drowned in the nearby lake. Some believe that an elemental – a supernatural entity manifested by occult means – which is associated with the corridors of the mansion, could be a remnant of those satanic rituals from the '70s.

What we see today when entering this magnificent structure is the potential for what could have been. Beautifully crafted cornices and ceiling arches, fireplaces left suspended in mid-air – where floors were never completed – and doorways which lead nowhere. In short, the place oozes character and charm.

But it also harbours a tragic past.

The Airman in the Attic

Woodchester Mansion acted as a base for American and Canadian troops between 1939 and 1945, who utilised the adjoining lake as a training site for bridge-building in preparation for the D-Day landings in Normandy, scheduled to take place on 6 June 1944.

Legend has it that several soldiers lost their lives in the murky waters following the collapse of one of the pontoons. Their bodies were stored in the coldest part of the mansion – the game larder – for some time, stacked unceremoniously upon each other and surrounded by the dead animals from the day's hunting.

Many believe they are responsible for some of the strange noises heard around the building at night, particularly in the bathroom on the second floor, where much of the planning for their exercises took place.

Many visitors and paranormal investigators have described hearing vintage music within the mansion, but on 27 March 2010 one ghost hunter captured something seemingly quite staggering; not auditory, but on a digital camera's SD card.

It was a particularly cold night with crisp, cloudless skies, and a bright moon which bathed the mansion in an eerie glow.

During a public ghost hunt with Haunted Happenings, one of the guests took the opportunity to carry out a solo investigation of the very sinister and foreboding corridor on the upper floor.

This area of the building is particularly unnerving; a spiral, stone staircase offering the only escape should one experience something frightening up there.

One guest who attended that night recalls vividly how the events unfolded when the volunteer made a shocking discovery.

"It was my first ever ghost hunt. As I remember the guy was a sceptic and therefore had no fear in sitting alone in that corridor when a volunteer was called for to hold a lone vigil.

Everyone else took a break and it was only when we went upstairs to do a vigil ourselves that we discovered him still sitting on the chair.

We spoke with him and he told us about an odd photograph he'd taken. He said it was a new camera and he'd been playing around with the settings, and this particular image seemed to reveal someone in the room with him."

The image in question appears to show the profile of a man's face. In the darkness of the corridor the pale, gaunt outline of the features are visible, with a dark shadow around the head which, upon inspection, creates the impression that the figure is wearing a hat or a cap.

The detail is so spectacular that it even appears to show a pair of spectacles upon the face, and the white of the man's bared teeth from an almost sneering smile.

The date and time stamps of the images were checked and were found to be in sequence, yet those either side of it revealed nothing other than the dark corridor in which the guest was taking the photographs.

He was definitely alone up there!

It's always important when scrutinising evidence of potential paranormal activity to remain impartial, and avoid the temptation to make things 'fit' just to suit the story.

However, many of those who have seen the now infamous photograph have commented that the head gear bears a distinct similarity to the Canadian aviation hat famously associated with the fictional pilot and adventurer, Biggles.

In light of the mansion's history and its connection with the Canadian troops, it seems startling that the image should so closely resemble one such character.

Did the ghost of an airman reveal himself on camera that night?

I would certainly like to hope so!

A Voice from the Grave?

For any paranormal investigator, capturing irrefutable evidence is always the goal. The internet is overflowing with images claiming to show real ghosts, but as technology advances it becomes increasingly difficult to identify genuine articles from clever fakes.

But capturing ghostly activity on film is only one of many ways to search for proof of spirits and ghosts, and on 22 July 2016, a visiting paranormal group from the USA were sound recording a vigil in the cellars of Woodchester Mansion, when something truly terrifying happened.

The night was another public ghost hunt with Haunted Happenings, and the evening was not long underway.

With a health and safety brief conducted in what would be our base room for the night, it was decided that the whole group would make their way straight down into the cellars, where our psychic medium would attempt to offer information regarding the energies she sensed at that time.

Whilst it wouldn't be the intention to focus purely upon contact with one particular spirit throughout the night, it can be helpful to gain a psychic perspective about any entities which may be present at the time, and therefore give the group the opportunity to experience something together, before splitting off into smaller teams for the rest of the ghost hunt.

With an overview of the mansion's history already digested, we gathered in the corridor of the cellars and prepared to attempt our first contact with the dead.

This area of Woodchester Mansion is one of those most feared by those who take part in ghost hunts here. Descending the wooden staircase into the bowels of the mansion alone is a foreboding experience, and as you turn right into the darkness which awaits, one is faced with a long passageway, off which a series of archways lead into smaller side rooms.

The walls of the cellar are constructed of large stone blocks, with an arched brickwork ceiling above. A mixture of sand and earth covers the ground under foot, and when all lights are extinguished the whole area is plunged into the depths of blackness; the only respite being the soft glow from the moon on a clear night, seeping through tiny openings in the smaller rooms to the sides.

Having conducted many vigils down here before, I decided to request that the group link hands for this first vigil. The purpose of this is twofold.

Firstly, it's generally accepted that spirits harness the energy of those around them to initiate contact, drawing power from the living in order to make those noises and displays of light which we often request of them. By connecting everyone's hands together it is theorised that the energy could be greater, and therefore increase the likelihood of us witnessing something paranormal.

Secondly, if everyone's hands are linked together, then should anyone report the sensation of being touched or grabbed during the vigil, it would be easier for them to accept that the person either side of them were not playing games, since they would have contact with their hands at all times.

With one or two pieces of equipment placed upon the floor in the hope of detecting any fluctuations in EMF (electromagnetic fields), we commenced calling out for contact.

Our medium that night had begun to sense a presence within the room, and one or two guests had already reported hearing faint noises for which we couldn't identify the source.

It was fortunate for us that the American team of investigators had decided to join in with this initial vigil before breaking away to do their own investigation, as they brought with them a recording device, in the hope of capturing any other-worldly noises during the night.

Despite having a number of experienced ghost hunters and

paranormal investigators in the group that night, none of us were quite prepared for what was about to unfold.

A short while into the vigil, three people who had their backs to an entrance on the left side of the corridor began to feel uneasy; sensing a presence of someone or something behind them.

Our medium was standing next to them and, in order to ensure I could access a light immediately – should someone become unwell or afraid – I remained in the centre of the circle, just a few feet away from the archway. We continued to call out for the spirits of the mansion to make contact.

And then it came.

Without warning, the loudest exhale of a man's breath filled the room, echoing throughout the corridor. It was a guttural sound, seemingly emitted from the very pit of the stomach and, in the darkness, quite terrifying.

The sound had come from over my left shoulder, and although impossible to say for sure, it had seemed incredibly close to my left ear.

In an instant I had clicked the button on my torch, only to be faced with the terrified faces of those in the doorway rushing towards me, hands still gripping each other in fear.

The room filled with the screams of those who heard the sound, soon turning into a babble of voices, all trying to discover what had caused the sudden rush of fear.

As someone with a very balanced view of the paranormal and, dare I say it, a relatively sceptical mind, my immediate thoughts were that one of the men in the room must have made the sound and was denying it for whatever reason.

However, as I pieced the scene together in my mind and tried to restore calm so that we could return to the vigil and attempt further contact, I realised something horrifying. The only people close to me in that cellar when the noise came were women. There were no men immediately to my left and yet the breath –

deep and masculine – had been very clearly from a man.

To experience a sound so menacing in the darkness a haunted building is a dream for some, and a nightmare for most.

Thankfully, although distant because of their position within the room, the sound was captured by the paranormal team, and has been retained as part of their investigation of the night.

On that balmy summer's night in the basements of Woodchester Mansion, I am convinced that twenty seven people were confronted with something, or someone, from the other side, and I can say with all honesty, it is not an experience I ever wish to repeat.

The Man in the Moonlight

Many years prior to the encounter in the cellars – barely a year into my foray as a ghost hunter – I was fortunate to experience what I would consider to be my first sighting of a ghost. Not the wispy-white figure of a woman so often depicted in the movies, nor the fully formed image of a child in Victorian clothing, but a silhouette. The outline of a man. But what really is a ghost?

Understanding the difference between a ghost and a spirit is important when taking part in a ghost hunt or paranormal investigation.

A spirit is considered to be the very essence of our soul. That unique and identifiable thing which makes us who we are. That which we either love or loathe about a person and what makes us human.

Several scientific experiments have been carried out over the years in an attempt to prove that when we die our spirit leaves the body, and continues to exist in some way – as energy.

Photographs are plentiful on the internet which show a wispy blur hovering above a body at the time of death, either white or greyish in colour.

The 21 grams experiment was a study in 1907, in which a physician by the name of Duncan MacDougall hypothesised that the soul of a person carries a physical weight. He measured the weight of six people just before and after the moment of death, and concluded that one had lost 21.3 grams in the process of passing over.

Although the experiment is considered flawed due to the small number of subjects examined, it is a theory which has since gained some support.

It is with spirit that many ghost hunters believe it's possible to communicate on a conscious and intelligent level.

In contrast, a ghost is merely the image of a figure from a previous time; someone from the past who – for reasons unknown – is visible to us in the present on certain occasions.

It's not fully understood how or why this phenomena is thought to occur, although theories include the possibility that buildings can absorb energy from the past and – given the right combination of factors – replay the image in future times.

In a similar way to a VHS recording being played over and over again, it's believed by many that particularly happy or traumatic events can leave an imprint on the building or land, which is effectively playing on a loop, and may be witnessed again in the future – given the right combination of dates, times and even lunar cycles.

As human beings we are composed of energy. The daily routine of getting out of bed, walking down the stairs and opening the door to let the dog out is a repetitive action, one which it is theorised *could* leave a lasting imprint of our energy upon the very fabric of the house in which you live.

Therefore, when people talk of witnessing a ghostly figure walk through a wall, or appearing to levitate two feet above the ground, it is possible they are simply going about their business and entering a doorway which is no longer there, or walking on a floor which has long since been lowered by several feet.

A ghost is thought to be nothing more than a replay of something from the past, with no awareness of us and no ability to communicate.

For that reason, I believe that in the corridor leading to the rear entrance to Woodchester Mansion, I saw a ghost.

It was around 12.10am and the ghost hunt was well underway. The night had been quiet thus far, with little more than the odd unexplained sound, and one or two reports of light anomalies in different parts of the mansion.

As the groups switched around, so that everyone had the opportunity to experience the building as a whole, I gathered my new team just outside the entrance to the kitchen.

From our position we could look straight down two corridors; one looking backwards towards the steps leading to the cellars, and the other leading to the rear entrance of the mansion.

At the junction on which we stood we had a clear line-of-sight in both directions, and it was when I briefly shone the torch toward the doorway, to give the group some perspective on our position within the building, that it happened.

One of the female guests and I saw somebody walk across the corridor; the figure of a man silhouetted perfectly in the moonlight, which cascaded through the open doorway beyond. In a split second I returned the torchlight to the spot, expecting to see one of the group walking towards us.

There was nobody there!

The person we had both just witnessed had disappeared without trace!

Instinctively we ran towards the place where the figure had been just seconds before, presuming to find somebody who had strayed from another vigil, yet all we found was an empty hallway.

During a public ghost hunt each of the smaller teams will break off into different parts of a building; areas carefully selected to minimise noise pollution during the vigils, and to reduce the chances of mistaken sightings.

Due to the sheer scale of Woodchester Mansion the three groups were working far apart; one on the upper floor, one in the cellar, and then ours, in the downstairs corridor. The only other person in the building at the time was the guy who opened and closed the mansion for us, and we later confirmed that he was in the drawing room with his headphones on, immersed in watching a horror film on his laptop while we investigated the mansion.

Having checked the whole area on the ground floor and outside the doorway, we compared notes on what we had seen.

Both agreed that we had seen a figure, around 6ft in height, walk at pace across the end of the corridor leading from the Chapel area of the mansion.

The figure had crossed the doorway at quite some speed and with real purpose, arms swinging as it passed – in a similar fashion to that of a marching soldier.

With an unobstructed view down the corridor, a living person could only have turned towards us or away from us, in which case they would have remained visible, as the torchlight was only taken away for the briefest moment.

As we moved around the area in an attempt to find an answer for what we had witnessed something else dawned upon us.

There had been no sound.

No footsteps were heard with the movement of the figure, yet the flooring at the time comprised of small pieces of gravel, making it impossible to navigate without making the familiar crunching sound underfoot.

In addition, directly opposite the corridor leading from the Chapel there is a flight of stairs, but upon further inspection we discovered that the wooden gate which sits across these steps was padlocked and – even if it were not – the gate opens outwards, meaning that a living person could not have made it up the stairwell in the brief second between us seeing the figure and returning the torchlight to the space.

I have visited the mansion multiple times since this encounter, but have never witnessed the same thing again. However, every time I walk through the Chapel and retrace the steps this figure would have made that night, I am unable to turn right, towards the doorway, without checking to my left first.

Whoever we saw in the moonlight at Woodchester Mansion that night will forever remain a mystery, although one of the most commonly reported sightings in the building is that of a dark, Monk-like figure on the ground floor around the Chapel.

Were we fortunate enough to witness the manifestation of the infamous Brother Michael who is said to have drowned on the estate? Did we observe one of the soldiers, whose body was kept in a room off this very corridor, marching once again?

Only Woodchester Mansion knows the answer to those questions, and I suspect it will never reveal its secrets.

THE DANA PRISON
Shrewsbury – Shropshire

They hang us now in Shrewsbury jail:
The whistles blow forlorn,
And trains all night groan on the rail
To men that die at morn.

– A.E Housman –

In the United Kingdom we are fortunate to have an exciting and rich tapestry of historic buildings to explore, from medieval castles to ancient inns, and everything in between. But few places retain the absolute authenticity which Shrewsbury Prison – known commonly as 'The Dana' – affords its visitors.

So many historic buildings have been developed into tourist attractions, or adapted for use as conference centres, thus chipping away at the fabric of their soul.

Although now used as the setting for a number of immersive themed-events and educational tours, The Dana Prison has remained essentially unchanged since the day the prisoners were shipped out and the gates closed for the final time.

There has been a correctional institution on the site since 1793, when the original Georgian prison was built. The current Victorian building was constructed upon those existing foundations in 1877, in close proximity to the place where a gruesome medieval Gaol once existed.

The prison sits in the shadow of the historic Shrewsbury Castle, the two being separated by a railway line which cuts directly through the town and crosses the river beyond. One built to keep people out, the other to keep them in.

Many commuters passing through Shrewsbury train station are unaware of the presence of the disused Platform 8 – used to transport prisoners from The Dana for over forty years – now masked from the platform opposite by a high wall. A real-life ghost platform.

The prison's proximity to the railway is mentioned in the aforementioned stanza, taken from 'A Shropshire Lad' – a collection of sixty-three poems by A.E Housman, published in 1896.

In total seventy-one executions took place behind the walls of The Dana Prison between 1795 and 1961, the first of which was carried out on 15 August 1795, when John Smith was hanged for stealing ten cotton handkerchiefs.

During the 19th century fifty-eight men and two women were executed here, many for what we now consider relatively minor crimes; the final hanging taking place at 08:00hrs on 9 February 1961, when the hatch fell away beneath the twenty-one year old George Riley.

He was given a drop of just six feet and four inches.

He died instantly.

Crowds would gather outside the front of the prison to watch the spectacle of public executions, until a hanging shed was built against the back wall of the courtyard.

At some point in the early 20th century a new condemned suite was constructed next to the women's wing, and remained in use until the final execution in the 1960s.

Since The Dana became popular with ghost hunting enthusiasts in 2015, a number of unexplained occurrences have been reported from within the walls of the condemned suite, and it was in this very room – on Saturday 27 August 2016 – that something chilling happened.

Don't Tempt Me

With another ghost hunting event at HMP Shrewsbury looming, I had taken the decision to broadcast a lone vigil via Facebook from cell 23 on the ones (the name given for the ground floor of a prison). This particular cell had been a hotspot for activity on a number of previous occasions, and seemed like the perfect place to share with the viewers.

But the prison, it seemed, had other plans!

With the rest of the team and the staff members from the building all safely accounted for in the base room (the old visiting suite), I headed off to cell 23 to begin the broadcast. However, I quickly discovered that the data signal on my mobile would be insufficient to sustain a Facebook live from A-Wing, so I set about finding an alternative place.

With the upper landings of the wing offering no improvement, and C-Wing faring no better, my final option was the hanging room – an unsettling distance from the safety and support of the rest of the team, but enough signal to make the broadcast.

Haunted Happenings' team members will often broadcast live to Facebook from the many locations they investigate, and on this night I had planned to carry out a detailed investigation of the hanging room, giving members of the public the opportunity to watch from the comfort of their homes, and hopefully witness something interesting.

A number of trigger objects and EMF meters were placed around the room in the hope they would be moved or triggered during the investigation, which may indicate something paranormal was happening.

In addition, I was armed with a FLIR thermal-imaging device, which would identify any significant heat sources in the room while the investigation took place.

Having begun the live-feed and explaining to the viewers what was happening – along with a little information about the room itself – I began to attempt contact with the spirits who might still haunt this place.

A short while into the vigil I was drawn to a loud bang which clearly emanated from C-Wing – originally the women's section of the prison, but later reserved for vulnerable prisoners such as members of the police force, sex offenders and serving prison officers; basically anybody who would have been in serious danger in general population.

With one or two spikes of electromagnetic energy from the meters in the execution room, things seemed to be beginning to happen, but I couldn't ignore the noise from C-Wing, which sounded very much like a cell door banging twice; once loudly and then a second, softer bang.

Knowing the team well and that none of them would compromise the investigation by entering the building, I felt sure they had all remained in the base room, and that I was therefore the only living soul in the main block of the prison.

With trepidation I made my way towards the door which leads back to the wing, passing the condemned cell as I went.

In the foreboding darkness I called out for a few moments from the landing of C-Wing to anyone who may be present, but no further noises were heard. Suddenly the enormity of what I was doing dawned upon me.

I'm alone in a haunted prison and hearing noises.

Upon returning to the scene of the executions I believed I heard the chuckle of a man's voice – seemingly from over my left shoulder – near the window overlooking the main gateway.

The room was dark and eerily quiet. The only light was the glow from the mobile device, the thermal camera and a laptop screen, which had been placed on the floor in the exact spot where the condemned would stand in preparation for the impending drop.

The laptop was recording audio from the whole vigil for later analysis.

With viewers commenting that they had witnessed a figure standing behind me in the room, and others asking me to pose particular questions to the spirits, I called out in the hope of a response.

Pointing the thermal imaging device into total blackness, towards the entrance of the room, I continued the vigil.

'If there's anybody in this room with me, please could you walk towards this object that I'm holding?'

With no apparent thermal changes I continued asking.

'Can you walk towards it? I may be able to see you. Come and step towards me'.

Despite a few noises and fluctuations of the EMF meters, all seemed quiet. So, with the guests beginning to arrive outside for the overnight ghost hunt, I said my goodbyes and ended the broadcast.

However, it was a couple of days later that I made a discovery from the laptop audio which sent a chill down my spine.

Reviewing audio from an investigation is a laborious task. It involves hours upon hours of listening intently to the recording, trying to eliminate external influences and consider rational explanations for any sounds which appear out of the ordinary.

Having had it confirmed by the team that I was definitely alone in the building the whole time (the two prison staff members were also in the base room watching the live feed), I was thrilled and unnerved in equal measure to hear the whisper of a man's voice on the recording, just as I paused between sentences.

It chills me to this day when I listen to the words. Three clear syllables, whispered by an unseen voice in the darkness of the execution room.

'Don't tempt me!'

The words were not audible on the live broadcast, yet seemed relatively clear on the recording from the laptop, which was positioned around 8ft from where I was standing.

In light of my request for the spirits to walk towards me just moments earlier, the phrase seemed menacing and full of intent.

I'm not sure how I would have reacted had I heard the whisper while I was in the room, knowing that I had a long walk – past rows of empty cells with open doors, in utter blackness – to reach the comfort of my colleagues in the base room.

Would I have ran? Would I have challenged whoever it was that spoke to me? I'll never know.

But there's one thing of which I'm now certain in my own mind; there is definitely something out of the ordinary within those four walls.

Whistle down the Wing

With an increasing number of technical gadgets on the market for ghost hunters to employ during investigations, it's easy to overlook our own basic senses when attempting to make contact with the other side. From K2 and EDI meters, to EVP recorders and infra-red recording devices, there are literally hundreds of pieces of equipment available online, which a serious paranormal investigator may see as 'must haves' for their kit.

However, there is no ghost hunting device on the market

which can see, hear, taste, touch and smell. There is nothing quite as attuned and complex as the human body.

For example, your eyes are made up of more than two million working parts, and are capable of processing 36,000 pieces of information per hour. Your skin contains more than four million sensory receptors. You can smell approximately 10,000 distinct scents and are capable of picking up the scent of fear and disgust.

These are just some of the scientifically proven abilities you possess as a human being – all of which could prove invaluable when taking part in a ghost hunting investigation.

But there is more!

It's thought by some that the human body has an invisible energy field surrounding it, which is detectable to others. Some would call this an aura, and many believe that it's possible to sense people's emotions and personality traits based upon the aura they exude.

In simple terms, imagine walking into a room to be met by a married couple who greet you with a warm smile and portray the picture of happiness, and yet you 'feel' uncomfortable.

Something is wrong!

You know instinctively that you've interrupted an argument, despite protests to the contrary.

Have you ever met somebody new and had that feeling that you 'just don't like them'? That gnawing sensation in your gut, telling you there's something unsettling or odd about the person, although their actions do nothing to make you feel this way.

As human beings we are all capable of sensing energy and converting this into feelings; unsubstantiated instincts about a person or situation which you just cannot put your finger on, yet know you are right.

Your senses are rarely wrong!

So why are we so quick to overlook these amazing abilities

when searching for ghosts and spirits, in favour of relying upon electrical devices to alert us to a presence? The answer is possibly because we don't trust ourselves, and our senses cannot be used as proof to others!

Perhaps herein lies the problem with a paranormal investigation which relies purely upon gadgets, versus a ghost hunt with people seeking personal, sensory experiences.

Stories of ghosts and spirits have continued to be told for generation upon generation, with hundreds of thousands of people believing they have seen or sensed something paranormal in their life. These encounters often consist of sightings of ghosts, or of hearing strange noises.

Just because they were not captured on film or recorded on a device, does it mean they never happened?

Maybe we are just much more complex than any of the equipment yet produced. Perhaps it is the combination of a multitude of different senses which has allowed us to experience communication with the other side? Maybe there is an intrinsic link between energies, which makes it so much easier for a spirit who once walked the earth to communicate with a person who still does, as opposed to them using man-made energy as a source.

We just don't know!

However, one thing I feel quite sure about is that our senses are the best tool we have on any investigation into the paranormal, and this was certainly the case during a ghost hunt on one of the wings at The Dana Prison.

C-Wing was originally the female wing of the prison, housing women convicts until 1922, when it became home to vulnerable prisoners and sex offenders until March 2013, when the final inmates left for good.

This particular wing was not a place that the officers would relish working; especially the night shift. Only one officer would be on duty on the wing at night, and for security reasons they would be locked in, and would be required to radio for assistance if it were needed.

A number of former officers and prisoners have talked about strange experiences in this part of the prison, and two different ghosts are said to have been seen on regular occasions.

The first, a woman in white, is said to be seen walking from the end cell of the upper landing, towards the execution room at the opposite end of the wing.

Said to have been seen by prison staff and inmates alike, this would be chilling to witness in any environment, never mind a building into which you are locked, with no hope of escape.

A second figure has allegedly been seen sitting at the bottom of the staircase nearest to the condemned suite. This figure is said to be that of a small child, and is thought to perhaps have been connected to the earlier Georgian prison, the remnants of which lie just a few feet beneath C-Wing itself.

Many Haunted Happenings guests have walked into this wing and, for reasons unexplained, immediately felt uneasy – without prior knowledge of its history or the stories of its ghosts.

During one ghost hunt this wing was the scene of some truly spectacular activity, for which we never found the cause.

While escorting a group of roughly twenty people around the building to reveal a little history and begin some initial group vigils, we decided to whistle and request that the spirits repeat our sound. At the time the whole group was standing in a circle in the same area (around halfway along the wing), and then something unexpected happened.

The sound was returned from the far end of the block! A clear whistle, at almost the same pitch as ours, and far away from any of the group.

It's rare to experience such instant and clear auditory phenomena, and naturally this raised the excitement of those present.

So with everyone standing completely still, the whistle was repeated and a request made for it to be copied again.

We listened intently.

Again, from the same area of the building, the sound was returned.

It is important to understand and consider any potential external influences which could be misinterpreted during an investigation, and it was quickly pointed out that the train station is just a few hundred yards away – across the prison walls – and therefore we could potentially have heard a train screeching on the rails into the station.

However, having heard the same sound twice, almost instantly after us requesting the noise, we were intrigued.

The group moved further towards the end of the wing – nearer to where the noises seemed to be coming from – and we continued the vigil.

No fewer than five times in the space of ten minutes the whistle was heard, yet once we had moved our position it seemed to move too.

It was quite staggering to all those who heard it, and to this day I have never encountered such amazing results when trying to communicate with spirit through sounds.

It was later confirmed with the other team that nobody had joined us in the main building at the time, and therefore this strange phenomena in C-Wing has forever remained a mystery.

The Governor's Office

Tucked away at the far end of A-Wing, through a small network of corridors, lies the Governor's office; a large room with a bay window overlooking the gatehouse, with a smaller office attached.

Vertical blinds hang lifelessly from the rails above the bay.

The corridor walls leading to the office are covered with heavily embossed wallpaper, in stark contrast to the whitewashed brick and bright blue flooring of the wings. Inside, an empty fireplace – once adorned with thank-you cards to the Governor from relatives and prisoners alike – stares vacantly into the room.

The soul of this room is gone; its purpose stripped away with the transfer of the prisoners.

Due to the sheer scale of The Dana the Governor's Office is often overlooked during ghost hunting events. Naturally most visitors to this Victorian institution want to soak up the atmosphere in the guts of the prison; the harsh wings and the place where the executions were carried out.

However, on the night of Friday 12 May 2017 we made the decision to include this forgotten room, and focus our attention upon it throughout the night. A number of people reported feeling strange emotions in the office itself, and several EMF spikes were registered throughout the vigils, particularly from the adjacent room where, presumably, the Governor's assistant would have worked.

But it was during a table tipping séance in the office itself that something inexplicable occurred; what those present believed to have been a ghost from the past.

Table tipping is just one of the more traditional experiments often conducted during overnight ghost hunts.

Working on the basis that we are just massive bundles of energy ourselves, it's generally considered that the living can act as a source of energy for the dead; a rechargeable battery from which they can generate the ability to communicate with us.

With this in mind, table tipping involves the participants connecting their collective energy with one object – in this case a folding wooden table – and requesting that the spirits use that energy to knock on, or move the table.

As with all experiments involving physical contact there's a huge amount of trust required, and the potential for the ideomotor response to take effect – a highly-researched and proven psychological phenomenon, wherein a subject makes motions unconsciously.

However, with each person's fingers very lightly touching the surface of the table, and torchlight making everyone's hands clearly visible to each other, the group set about trying to contact the spirits.

'Can you please try to copy this knock on the table?' one of the group began.

The request was followed with a soft, clear tapping sound and startled faces lit up the room with excitement.

'Thank you so much. Could you do it twice please?'

Tap, tap.

The results were clear and seemingly on command.

During this experiment, three or four people remained in the other office – attempting the same experiment – and it was those few who were about to witness something which baffled us for the remainder of the night.

The doorway into the darkened corridor beyond was halfway open, a deliberate action so that we could hear any sounds which may come from beyond the rooms.

The corridor directly outside the office leads away in three directions. Straight ahead takes you back towards C-Wing, and the location of the room into which those sentenced to hang would drop. To the left you are taken around a corner and back down to A-Wing, and if you turn right you are led through a large gate and heavy door, out into the courtyard facing the gatehouse.

While making attempts within the smaller office to obtain some movement with the table, somebody walked past the doorway; a human form, walking straight towards the gate and to the courtyard beyond.

The irony of witnessing ghostly figures and apparitions during a ghost hunt is that often, the very thing we are so actively seeking passes us by in plain sight. This was one of those cases!

When something seemingly completely ordinary happens, such as somebody casually walking past you, it doesn't attract attention. It is only when we begin to ask ourselves questions or process other information that it becomes strange.

So, when the figure of a person walking past a doorway is so clear to the naked eye (albeit in shadow because of the surroundings) then there is nothing immediately unusual. One generally just assumes this is a living person, and that is exactly what happened that night.

The guests assumed in the moment that the security guard or another guest from a different area had passed by the doorway. Well they did, until their logical mind began to ask questions.

Why was there no sound of footsteps on the floor?

How come I didn't hear the door open and close?

Why was the person walking around in the dark without a torch?

One by one these questions seeped into their minds, and suddenly we were dealing with a potentially different situation.

It only took a few seconds for alarm bells to start ringing, and one of the guests shouted through to the group in the next room.

'Is there anybody walking outside?'

There was nobody!

The view from the Governor's Office has a clear line-of-sight across the courtyard toward the Gatehouse; nobody was there, and yet that was the direction in which the mysterious figure was seen walking just seconds earlier.

From the doorway of the office there is an unobstructed view of the corridor leading back to C-Wing, and there was nobody in sight there either.

So, whoever it was who passed the office doorway had done so silently, opened and closed a heavy door without making a sound, and then was nowhere to be found just seconds afterwards.

I have found no records of similar sightings in this area of the prison, and there is absolutely no way of validating what we saw that night, but as ghost hunters none of that matters.

The experience was a personal one to those who bore witness to it, and is something that will never leave them.

The security guard later confirmed that he had not passed this part of the building during our vigils, and even if he had, how could he have done so on hard flooring without making a sound, then disappeared without a trace?

Whoever the black shadow was, or whatever its purpose for being there that night, we do not know.

Perhaps one day somebody else will encounter the figure and offer some answers, but until then it will remain one of HMP Shrewsbury's many unsolved mysteries.

-5-

WARWICK CASTLE
Warwick - Warwickshire

"Warwick Castle, built of the very centuries, cannot be expected to alter with time's 'brief hours and weeks' – at least, with so few of them as fall to one poor mortal's lot. From visit to visit, I find it as unchanged as the multiplication table." – Katherine Lee Bates

To trace your fingers through words and shapes carved into the stone of a building by prisoners during the English Civil War is an incredible connection to make with the past.

To stand in the very rooms where some of the most influential characters in our history have plotted against English kings, and changed the narrative of our country, is awe inspiring.

To marvel at the largest collection of armoury in the UK outside the Tower of London, to look upon Queen Elizabeth's riding saddle and handkerchief, or to gaze at the majesty of Queen Anne's impressive four-poster bed.

All of these things are possible at the imposing Warwick Castle; a great British monument, the very fabric of which has remained unchanged for hundreds of years.

As with many strategic locations in the UK, William I established a motte and bailey fort at Warwick in 1068, shortly after the Norman Conquest of 1066.

The structure we see today mostly dates from the mid-14th century onwards, culminating with the building of the Spy Tower and extension of the state rooms, in preparation for a royal visit from Elizabeth I.

The castle has fought off numerous attacks and sieges throughout its time, and suffered a devastating fire in 1871, which gutted the Great Hall and damaged many of the private apartments; but still it stands, heroic and defiant.

Now in the ownership of Merlin Entertainments, who have lavished over £6 million on the castle in renovations over the last ten years, it has become one of the top visitor attractions in the UK.

But what of its ghosts?

Naturally, with 950 years of torrid history one would assume that the castle has many stories to tell.

Major battles, the imprisonment of kings, treason and murder, all have a place within the walls of this medieval fortress, and one of the most well-known ghosts is that of Sir Fulke Greville – a renowned poet and playwright, and once owner of the castle.

Greville was gifted the dilapidated castle by James I in 1604, and remained there until his untimely death in 1628; murdered in London at the hands of Ralph Haywood, his manservant.

Rumours were rife of a physical relationship between the two, and when Haywood discovered the paltry sum left to him by Greville in his will, he stabbed his master savagely in the stomach, before turning the knife on himself.

Greville didn't die instantly from his injuries. Physicians treated him by packing the wound with pig fat, which soon turned rancid, resulting in an agonising death from the subsequent infection, some four weeks later. His body was returned to Warwick and laid to rest in the nearby Church of St Mary.

But it seems he may not be at rest, for his ghost is said to have been seen on many occasions, walking the corridors of a castle he once lovingly restored.

In the tower which housed his study and bedchamber, witnesses have reported fleeting glimpses of a figure watching from the corners of the darkened room, and spoken of the feeling of a sad presence around them.

But it was in the grounds of the castle, not the tower, where I believe the infamous ghost of Warwick Castle may have made his presence known one night in 2013.

Shadows of the Past

Warwick Castle has always been a favourite place of mine. As someone who truly appreciates the history of such a location, it is always a privilege to be asked to host a ghost hunt here, and in order to allow time for a cursory check of the location – to ensure all of the daytime visitor attractions have been shut down for the event – I arrive early, often around two hours before the guests themselves are due.

To have the opportunity to walk around this location alone is an experience few are fortunate to have, and is something I cherish every time I work there.

On this particular evening, another team member had arrived at a similar time, and while I worked my way through checking each of the areas in which we would later conduct our vigils, she roamed the castle herself, exploring the nooks and crannies of this spooky location.

Darkness had already fallen by 8.05pm, as I entered the room of Bear Tower, directly opposite the entrance to the Chapel which lies just across the courtyard.

Upon leaving the tower I spotted my colleague across the

way, walking past the external Chapel staircase, heading towards the undercroft which would serve as our base room for the night. At least I *assumed* the shadowy figure in the darkness was her.

Briefly checking the time on my mobile phone I looked away for just a couple of seconds, while continuing to walk in the direction of the base room to meet up with her and have a chat about the night ahead. When I looked up again, just seconds later, she had disappeared.

Naturally, since the person I'd seen had been walking towards that room, I assumed I would find her waiting for me inside; but she was nowhere to be found.

I waited in the undercroft and around ten minutes passed before she returned, with a revelation which sent a chill through my bones.

'I just called out to you from the corridor,' she announced, feigning mock sadness that I had ignored her, 'are you deaf?'

Looking puzzled I asked where she had seen me, knowing full well I'd been waiting in the undercroft for almost ten minutes for her to return.

'I was at the bottom of the steps leading back up to the courtyard and you walked past, heading towards the Chapel,' she continued.

'That wasn't me,' I answered, 'I've been in here for ages. It must have been the security guard walking past.'

'No, it wasn't him. I literally just talked .to him in the Kingmaker area, and he went in the other direction, to switch off the sound system in the Gaol.'

My mind was instantly drawn back to the figure I had seen a short while earlier.

'Did *you* walk past the Chapel about fifteen minutes ago?' I asked, somewhat nervous of the reply.

She hadn't!

She went on to explain that she'd been at the other end of the castle for quite some time, exploring the maze of mirrors at the base of Caesar's Tower, and the Kingmaker attraction which runs beneath the state apartments and Great Hall.

At no point had she passed by the steps leading to the Chapel. So who did?

A short phone call to the security guard confirmed that there were no other members of the daytime staff onsite. The only three people in the Castle at the time were himself and the two of us.

More importantly, the guard insisted he hadn't walked in that area of the castle either, having been in the office until just prior to their brief exchange in the Kingmaker attraction.

So who was the mysterious shadowy figure we had both seen, walking in the same direction, with just a short time between the sightings?

Through comparison of our accounts, it would seem that we had both seen the silhouette of a person walk past the steps leading to the chapel. Both had assumed it to be the other person, and had therefore thought nothing more of it at the time.

The sightings were within fifteen minutes of each other, at times when all three people onsite were accounted for in other areas of the building.

We were left baffled and bemused with the potential that we had both seen the same ghost – on the same night and in the same place – but at slightly different times.

A very rare incident.

Did we encounter the ghost of Sir Fulke Greville that night? Were we witness to a ghostly apparition of someone else? Could there have been an intruder onsite without the security guard's knowledge?

The frustrating thing is we will never know for sure, yet this experience is one of which we often reminisce upon, and will certainly never forget.

The Abandoned Séance

Attempts to communicate with the dead are nothing new to Warwick Castle, yet in times gone by it wasn't the visitors who indulged in this fascination; it was those who lived there.

The elite of Victorian society were renowned for their dalliances with the paranormal, and one particular resident of the castle was well-known for hosting lavish parties, which often culminated in a séance to contact the dead.

Francis Evelyn Greville, Countess 'Daisy' of Warwick, was a celebrated hostess and socialite who became involved in several extra-marital affairs with a number of powerful men. Such was her flirtatious reputation, she was the inspiration behind the popular music hall song '*Daisy, Daisy*'.

A long-term mistress of the Prince of Wales, who later became King Edward VII, she faced increasingly large debts, even attempting to secure the sale of the private letters sent to her by the now late King to rescue her dwindling coffers.

A High Court ruling ensured the letters were never released, but Daisy's time at the castle reportedly left a greater mark than just her naughty reputation.

In the late 1800s the renowned spiritualist Aleister Crowley regularly conducted séances at Warwick Castle, in a bid to summon ghosts of the past.

Crowley was feared by many because of his dalliances with the occult, yet Daisy Greville invited him to the castle on a number of occasions, and it's said that during one such meeting a vortex was opened in the Kenilworth bedroom – a thin veil between the living and the dead, which has never been closed.

In July 2016 a paranormal investigator visiting this very room during the daytime snapped a picture on her iPhone, which appeared to reveal the figure of a man standing near the window, in the reflection of an information board.

The castle security team later confirmed that there were no waxwork figures in that part of the room, and even checked

CCTV footage to confirm the lady was alone at the time the photograph was taken.

Many people believe that an abandoned séance, which left the vortex open, is one of the reasons for the extreme levels of paranormal activity now reported at Warwick Castle.

Mirror Mirror on the Wall

A concealed corridor above the Great Hall links the Kenilworth suite to the main bedrooms of Warwick Castle, and it is across this hallway – on a number of separate occasions – that strange visions have been witnessed in the mirrors which adorn the rooms and corridors.

These visions – whilst not linked by date, time or person – have one thing in common; a moustache.

Scrying is a centuries-old practice with foundations in the search for prophecy and revelation; a means of fortune telling, often involving a crystal ball or similar glassy material.

Gazing into a suitable surface in the hope of receiving messages or visions from beyond this world, it has secured its place within the ghost hunting arena in the form of mirror scrying – using a mirrored surface in a haunted building, in the hope of calling forth one of the spirits and requesting that they change the image to show themselves in the reflection.

Although there's no scientific basis for the practice, it is a technique which can deliver startling and sometimes disturbing results for those brave enough to participate.

Whether the images witnessed come from the subconscious mind, an overactive imagination, one's psychic ability, or the spirit world itself, there can be no denying that some of the visions have been incredible at best, and at worst, terrifying.

In a long corridor, off which a number of bedrooms containing genuine period furniture lead, there is one mirror in particular which has baffled a number of people on many occasions.

Using just a small amount of light with which to illuminate the facial features, both men and women alike have stood before the mirror, and been confronted by the face of a man staring back at them in the darkness. Although the details aren't always clear, one overriding feature has often been evident; a dark moustache in a very specific and recognisable style.

The shape has been described time after time – on different nights and by people who have never met – as the same one sported by Charlie Chaplin, Oliver Hardy and Adolf Hitler.

As a ghost hunter with a very inquisitive, yet sceptical outlook, I would often question the validity of mirror scrying, considering the strong possibility that, as humans, we simply make the shadows fit into something we wish or hope to see.

However, having helped a variety of people carry out this experiment across several investigations – spanning a number of years and using the same mirror each time – the repetition of something so specific begs the question, how?

How could so many people see the same thing without having any prior knowledge of those who have gone before them? Why does the same style of moustache keep appearing in this one particular mirror?

In a building where you are surrounded by Victorian-style furniture, artefacts and portraits, surely if suggestion were playing a part then one would conjure up a much fuller mane; curving upwards and twisted at the tips, as was much more typical of Victorian and Edwardian men.

But no. Time after time participants have described a toothbrush moustache; clipped vertical at the edges rather than the more typical, tapered or twisted style, and just a small width of 3-5cm across the top of the lip.

Whilst the person standing before the mirror may or may not always see the vision themselves, due to the level of concentration involved, it is common for others to gather around them in the background, so as to have the opportunity to scrutinize the images which appear.

It is important that this happens so that multiple witnesses can validate what they are seeing, and to ensure that the person involved doesn't just allow the eyes to wander and create their own shapes.

What the spectators won't experience however, are some of the strange sensations and feelings which seem to come with the manifestation of the visions. Those it seems are rarely felt by anyone other than the person whose features are being manipulated in the mirror.

One of the common sensations described by a number of people has been that of sadness. An overwhelming and all-consuming emptiness; the sort of hollow void normally only experienced by those who have lost someone close.

Grown men have been reduced to tears while carrying out the experiment in this mirror, and although we have no way of knowing who this vision could be, or the reason why these feelings seem to be projected onto the person doing the scrying, having witnessed the same phenomena happen time after time I genuinely believe that it has something to do with the castle, and perhaps one of the characters from its past.

Yet more strange is the vision which has appeared in another mirror nearby, situated in one of the larger bedrooms, next to the bathroom. Again, the same visions have been described by a number of people on different occasions, but this time the features seem to morph into something even more alarming, and seemingly not human.

When shadows fall upon the face at unusual angles it is very easy for the brain to misinterpret them and imagine the eyes have sunk inwards, the lips have narrowed, or even that a moustache has grown!

But why a person would describe the vision of a lion or cat's features being projected back at them I am completely at a loss to understand.

This was first mentioned sometime around 2012, but since then there have been at least four other occasions where people – normally women – have described particularly feline features forming before their very eyes. Very specifically, the results have been described as having a 'particularly pronounced brow', 'high cheeks' and even a 'curly mane'.

More than one of the participants have described the appearance as resembling the cowardly lion from the 1939 MGM classic *The Wizard of Oz*. A very unusual vision by any standards! Although maybe not quite so strange.

Following some research into the history of the castle it emerged that Charles Greville – 7th Earl of Warwick and the last Earl to live at the family seat of the castle before its sale in 1978 – moved to America and became the first British aristocrat to star in a Hollywood movie, under the stage name of Michael Brooke. Hollywood later nicknamed him the Duke of Hollywood and Warwick the Filmmaker (a pun on Warwick the Kingmaker).

During his time in Hollywood he was linked with a number of high-profile stars including Marlene Dietrich and Greta Garbo, and became well-known for socialising within celebrity circles.

Bearing in mind that description which was given more than once from the bedroom mirror of the cowardly lion's face, it is somewhat interesting that the studio he signed with in Hollywood was none other than MGM.

Of course this is a tenuous link, and we should be careful during any type of ghost hunting or paranormal investigation not to make connections for the sake of them, but is it possible that Greville was known to Bert Lahr – the actor who played the lion in the film?

Greville's career with MGM ended after just six months and

led to a lengthy court battle.

He died in January 1984 but perhaps his ghost lives on in the castle. Maybe the vision represents the acting stardom he craved, or the role he so coveted.

We will never know, and that – for all its frustrations – is one of the greatest joys of ghost hunting.

The Forgotten Tower

In 2013 Warwick Castle unveiled four previously unseen areas of their historic building; rooms which, until then, had never been accessible to members of the public.

One of those spaces had been hidden in plain sight for years, with thousands upon thousands of people walking right past its doorway since the castle became popular with visitors during the mid-19th century.

In the centre of the north-west curtain wall which surrounds the castle is a gateway, flanked on either side by a pair of towers; a 15th century addition to the fortifications.

Unlike Caesar's Tower and Guy's Tower, which dominate the town's skyline and loom ominously over the surrounding grounds, the Bear and Clarence structures – intended for use as defensive gun towers – were never completed; building was abandoned upon the death of King Richard III in 1485.

Little remains of the two unfinished fortifications other than their foundations and a small room. It's within this room, in the base of Bear Tower, that something strange seems to occur.

The room in Bear Tower measures little more than 5m x 5m, and when the door is closed behind you the lack of any natural light plunges visitors into absolute blackness, regardless of the time of day.

Inside, an arched brickwork ceiling curves overhead.

To enter the room one has to stoop through the doorway and walk across a metal grille, beneath which lies a cavernous pit –

thought to have been used by the castle's owners to cage the bears used for baiting; a cruel 'sport' symbolised in Warwickshire's coat of arms, the instantly recognisable ragged bear and staff.

This image dates back to Richard Neville – the infamous Kingmaker – who adopted it as his badge during the Wars of the Roses between 1455 and 1487, and has become intrinsically linked with Warwick Castle.

But the strange occurrences within the tower have nothing to do with this barbaric activity. It is something far stranger and more difficult to explain.

The first time we became aware of the sound was in 2013, just a short time after the room was unveiled to the public.

With a small group of ghost hunters gathered, we began what was our first proper investigation of the space. With no expectations of who or what might be encountered in the darkness, the group formed a circle and held hands while calling out for any spirits present to make themselves known in some way.

And that's when it happened.

The distinct sound of movement from above. Footsteps on wooden flooring. The dull thud of movement echoing into the blackness.

Thud, thud, thud.

Of course the first instinct in a situation like this is to eliminate the possibility that somehow those present in the room were creating the noise themselves, through slight movements on the wooden floor within the space.

Having taken all measures to attempt to recreate the sound, the group's attention turned to the exterior of the building.

A cursory check outside confirmed there was nobody up on the battlements above the room. In fact, access to the ramparts of the castle is prohibited during night-time investigations for safety purposes, making it impossible for anyone to stray onto the turret above.

Later examination of aerial photographs of the grounds revealed that the surface above is comprised of sturdy stone slabs; nothing that could create the hollow sounds heard by those within the room below.

Where are the noises coming from?

The sounds continued for several minutes. Periods of complete silence, followed by short bursts.

'Can you let us know you are here please?'

Thud, thud, thud...

Then silence.

'Can you do that again please?

Thud, thud, thud...

And so it continued.

To experience something so baffling in the company of a small number of like-minded people is a thrill. Quite simply, moments like this are the reason why ghost hunting intrigues so many people.

We could all hear the sounds. Nobody was moving within the room. But still they came!

Since that night this strange phenomena has happened on a number of occasions; each time the same sounds, but still no explanation has been found.

With each new event a new group of people who have never met. People who would have no prior knowledge of the incident in 2013, and therefore no preconception of what may or may not happen in this particular part of the castle.

But still it happens.

Thud, thud, thud... Movement from above.

Perhaps one day an answer will be found. Perhaps it won't.

Either way, the amazement on each and every person's face who is privy to this unknown activity continues to make me smile time and time again.

It would be a brave soul to sit alone in Bear Tower. The darkness is all-consuming. The atmosphere is sometimes oppressive. The sounds from above are unnerving.

But that's what we seek. Ghost hunters all around the world just want to know one thing…if anybody is there.

-6-

ALTON TOWERS
Alton - Staffordshire

Majestic. Imposing. Palatial. Alton Towers was once all of these things. But in 1952 the house was stripped to the bone for materials; its very soul torn apart. Now all that stands is a shell in the middle of the eponymous theme park.

Empty. Sad. Decaying.

Each year hundreds of thousands of thrill seekers pass through the gates of Alton Towers' theme park in Staffordshire. Roller coasters screech across the tracks. The screams of riders fill the air – mock terror expelled from their lungs mid-flight – and families soak up the fun like eager sponges.

It has become the UK's favourite theme park over a number of years, but few who come here for the rides take a moment to consider the building from which the park's name is derived.

Even fewer realise that the Gothic masterpiece which looms ominously over the lake has a dark and sinister reputation for paranormal activity, one which has left many people terrified and afraid to return.

But why is a particular building haunted?

This question is often asked and the simple answer is nobody truly knows. However, when you consider the history of the piece of land on which a property lies, you may find yourself peeling back layers upon layers of history; often chequered, sometimes morbid, and almost always longer than you'd initially imagine.

It can be easy to forget that what we see today is only the most recent incarnation of the land's history, and at Alton Towers this is very much the case.

The land which encompasses the Alton estate was once the site of an Iron Age fort, built on Bunbury Hill in the 1st century BC. In around 700AD the Saxon King Ceolred of Mercia built a fortress on the hill, and in the 11th century a fortified castle was erected soon after the Norman Conquest.

So why is this important?

Well, when you consider the possibility that each of these layers of history – often bloody through battle – have left their mark on the land, it begins to make sense.

The castle was destroyed during the English Civil War, but in the late 17th century the Talbot family redeveloped the site to create a hunting lodge for use as a summer residence.

Extensive renovations were carried out by Charles Talbot, the 15th Earl of Shrewsbury, and completed by his heir, John Talbot, sometime around 1830.

Charles' work on the lodge saw the addition of a drawing room, chapel, library, long gallery, conservatory, dining room, and the incredibly impressive banqueting hall. So extensive were the works that the building almost doubled in size, and the Gothic-style architecture we see today dates from this period.

In its heyday Alton Lodge was packed to the rafters with the finest things money could buy. Beautifully crafted furniture, exquisite drapes and expensive accessories were to be found in every corner of the building; a statement of wealth and importance which could not have gone unnoticed.

So how did it become the empty shell which ghost hunters now explore? Quite simply – money.

A legal battle over ownership of the estate resulted in much of the contents of the house being auctioned, and later – following the separation of the 20th Earl and his countess – much of the estate followed.

The countess continued to live there for two years after the Earl died, but the house fell into disrepair due to the extortionate running costs of such a large property, and it was eventually sold to a group of local businessmen in 1924, thus ending its turbulent history as the Talbots' family home forever.

Today the towers are open for the public to explore, but what a sad sight they are. Stripped right back to the stonework, the cavernous rooms are little more than a shadow of their past.

Vast window frames through which sunlight once radiated now act as open doorways for the harsh weather to penetrate the fabric of the building.

Beautifully carved stonework is being eaten away by damp, and in many areas the building is decayed beyond repair. However upsetting it may be for anyone with an appreciation of architecture and history to see a property befall such a fate, this is exactly the type of setting which excites those with a thirst to search for the paranormal.

And in recent years Alton Towers has become almost as famous for its ghosts as for its daytime attractions.

The Ring

"I'll believe in anything, no matter how outlandish it may seem to others. But the more crazy it may appear, the more evidence I'll want before I allow myself to believe."

It is probably fair to say that most people who take part in ghost hunting vigils are looking for validation. For some this may be proving to themselves that their scientific beliefs and principles are correct, and that there will always be a logical explanation for that which may at first appear out of the ordinary. For others it might be the desire to experience something first-hand which supports their belief that ghosts and spirits do exist.

Whatever the intention, we are all seeking something. But often, when the very thing we seek actually comes to fruition, we can sometimes struggle to make sense of it.

This was exactly the case when, on Saturday 27 February 2016, one man found himself dealing with something completely unexpected in a dark recess of the towers.

I've always believed that it is important to keep trying new things during a ghost hunt. New experiments. New ways of asking for contact. New incentives for spirit to actually bother talking to us.

However, I am also keen to ensure there is some control surrounding the experiments we try; some way of validating the things people report. Any way possible of removing doubt about what may have been experienced, and the avoidance of allowing suggestion or a 'me too' situation to arise.

For example. If two people were to witness something and one of them were to begin recounting their experience within earshot of the other, then the second person's recollection may be instantly influenced by that of the first, resulting sometimes in them believing something other than what they originally thought.

So, when conducting the vigils, I will usually try to put in place some mechanisms which help us to avoid such situations.

When conducting a Ouija board vigil, I will often enter four random digits into my mobile phone and place it far away from those involved in the experiment. Asking spirit to move towards the object and then try to find those shapes – the numbers on the board – will ensure that nobody could possibly influence the results.

The probability of guessing a four digit number are 1 in 10,000, so that's not going to happen during a ghost hunt is it?

Wrong!

On three separate occasions when attempting this control mechanism during a Ouija board experiment, all four numbers have been found on the board, with no possible way of the participants knowing the digits on the device.

How the hell does that happen?

I do not know.

So in the same vein – during a watch and wait vigil on the landing where a woman is said to have fallen from the building at Alton Towers – I requested that the guests try something unusual.

'If you'd like to take part can you please put your hands out before you, with your fingers spaced apart?' I began explaining to the guests. 'Now if you do feel anything during this experiment please don't say anything other than "me", so that I'm aware *if* we have had any response to my requests.'

By now there were one or two anxious looks from people, but I began calling out.

'If there is anybody here with us, could you please approach somebody you feel comfortable with, and choose a finger on one of their hands to touch?'

There were a few nervous giggles at this point, which I suppose is to be expected in the circumstances, but nobody reported feeling anything, so I continued.

'You can squeeze somebody's finger, try to pull it lightly, or even give it a little scratch. Just enough to let them feel you without hurting them.'

The idea behind this experiment is to hopefully give somebody in the group a personal interaction which they can be certain of; something that nobody can take away from them.

By keeping the lights off it helps to prevent people from inadvertently giving away any information about which finger they have felt any sensations on.

So, before turning on the lights to compare experiences, I normally ask anyone who has felt anything to take a step forward into the circle and hold the hand or finger in the air.

When the lights go up it's sometimes staggering to find that two, three, even four people sometimes have the same finger in the air – despite having no way of knowing what others had felt.

Even more strange is that sometimes they then describe the same type of feeling; a squeeze, a stroke, even a tingling sensation.

Of course it doesn't work every time. Despite the way it often appears on television these things rarely happen on cue, and it will often take a long time before anything of any note actually happens.

This was the case now; or so I thought at the time.

On that particular investigation I had been joined for the night by my partner, who was helping with the running of the event, and who had joined us for this tour of the building.

As team members with a ghost hunting company, we would always avoid mentioning to guests any of the experiences we have ourselves, for fear it may appear we were trying to influence their experience.

Understanding the importance of this, it was only when we returned to the base room that he informed me what had happened to him during that earlier vigil.

Here's the story he shared with me, in his own words.

"I'd only tagged along with the group because I wanted to see the building, and hadn't planned on taking part in any of the experiments. But when they asked everyone to put their hands out in front of them I just followed suit, without even thinking of the potential consequences.

Nobody felt anything the first couple of times when people asked for the spirits to try touching someone's hand, and to be honest I never expected it to. But then the weirdest thing started to happen.

It was a pretty cold night anyway, and the breeze which came through the open window frames was biting, but my right hand suddenly felt really odd. It wasn't necessarily any colder, but it sort of tingled – like that feeling when you get pins & needles.

The group kept asking for something to happen and that's when I felt it.

I wear a tungsten ring on the fourth finger of my right hand, and even when my hands are cold it doesn't tend to move or slide down my finger. However, I noticed that just after the tingling had started on that hand, the ring started to move on its own.

It wasn't just slipping down my finger as you might expect if it was loose, but it was actually turning – just like you do when you're trying to remove a ring which is a bit tight.

I'll be honest and say that I froze for a second, partly because it freaked me out, but also because I didn't want to make it look like I was saying something was happening just because nobody else was feeling anything.

The turning happened for a few seconds, and by the time I moved my hands back into my pockets it had moved forwards a few centimetres, all the way down to my knuckle.

I'd never experienced anything I'd consider paranormal before that night, not really, and it freaked me out for a while.

Standing in the dark, knowing that someone or something is touching you, is a freaky experience.

I've been on a few ghost hunts since that night, but whenever they do this experiment now I keep my hands firmly in my pockets where they're safe – and warm."

It's exactly this type of personal encounter which truly affirms in a person's mind that something strange has happened which will probably never be explained.

Don't Look Back

Walking through a vast building like Alton Towers can be a daunting experience. Knowing that you are completely alone in this sprawling mansion is both exhilarating and creepy. But when you add to this the sheer blackness of a moonless winter sky, and an unexpected encounter mid-way down a spiral staircase, the whole episode becomes utterly terrifying.

But why would anybody be daft enough to venture alone into a reputedly haunted building, with nobody around to hear them scream?

Exposure therapy has been used for many years to help people with genuine phobias overcome their fears.

Continued and escalated exposure to the very thing which a person is afraid of, gradually builds a certain level of immunity to the fear.

The only way to become more confident with presenting to a crowd of people is to practice. Start with small groups and gradually build to larger audiences. Over time it will become less daunting and, in time, the fear will dissolve into little more than butterflies in the stomach.

For anyone who regularly spends time in dark, reportedly haunted places – with only torchlight for company – fear gradually dissipates over a period of time.

Shadows are generally accepted as simply tricks of the light, distant bangs are presumed to be nothing more than a car door closing somewhere nearby, and those tickling sensations people often report when spirit is nearby are taken as probably nothing more than a spider's web.

In a sense we become immune over time, and less inclined to allow our imagination to run away with us when placed in a situation which many would find uncomfortable.

In short – ghost hunters don't tend to get carried away and believe every little noise is something paranormal.

But every now and then something happens which just doesn't 'feel' right, and in those moments we can run from a building just as fast as anyone else.

On this particular night, in March 2013, the towers looked especially eerie. The gothic structure was shrouded in a hazy fog which floated densely across the lake, and there was a bitterness in the air which nipped at the bare flesh of the hands and face.

I had arrived earlier than expected due to lighter than normal traffic on the motorway, and wasn't expecting the first of our team to arrive for at least another thirty minutes.

The Alton Towers security team had allowed me into the grounds, and after quickly setting out all the equipment I'd need for the night ahead, I decided to take a walk through the building.

For me, one of the most exhilarating rewards of hosting ghost hunting experiences with Haunted Happenings is the unprecedented access we often have to these amazing and historic places.

To be in a position to walk alone through such an imposing and impressive building – one that most will only ever experience while in the company of thousands of other daytime visitors to the park – is a thrill.

Although very logical in thought, and still relatively sceptical about what really causes 'paranormal' activity, I will always do whatever I can towards helping the guests increase their chances of an experience.

So, with that in mind, I made the decision to enter the building alone and walk through its many rooms and corridors, to begin communication with anyone who might be listening through the thin veil between this world and the next.

Basically, I wanted to 'warm the spirits up' before we got

started.

I've always worked on the basis that you need to be interesting as a person if you wish to gain somebody's attention – whether they're alive or already dead.

Being creative with the questions we use is critical during a ghost hunt.

Understanding some of the history of a building, finding out about key events which may still be of interest to those who once lived or worked there, or even just playing music from a period of time which may entice one of the spectral residents from the shadows and encourage them to make contact with you.

It makes sense to me that these are the surely the best ways to pique somebody's interest and get them to come forward.

Walking down the cast-iron staircase into the underbelly of the building, I had a flutter of excitement – or was it nerves?

Wandering into one or two rooms of a haunted building while knowing that your team mates are nearby is one thing, but on this occasion I was literally the only living person in the grounds of the estate (except for the security guard who was roughly a quarter of a mile away in the gatehouse).

I could feel the thumping of my heart as I descended into the dark, damp corridor which leads to the kitchens (an area where – on a number of previous occasions – a sinister presence has been felt).

Taking the staircase into the Banqueting Hall, I then exited through the long gallery and into what was once the music room – a cavernous space now devoid of the joyous sounds which would once have pervaded the air.

Pausing for a few moments, I reached for my phone, selected the music app, and pressed play. In a second the sweet lyrical sounds of Schubert's 'Trout Quintet' began to fill the otherwise empty space, seeping into the very cracks of the stonework.

In an instant the room felt different.

I imagined for a moment those occasions when chamber music would have filled the space, and after a short while began calling out for any spirits who may recognise the piece to come forward tonight, and make themselves known to the group when they arrived.

I didn't notice any sounds or changes within the area, so proceeded to climb the wooden staircase to the upper floors, where the spectral figure of a woman in black has been reported an a number of occasions.

From the top of these stairs it's possible to ascend to the rooftop, via a narrow spiral staircase.

Just like in any good horror film, when one of the characters makes the decision to venture into the attic or a darkened basement, anyone watching me at the time would have been screaming for me not to enter – but bravado led me to ignore common sense and climb the stairs regardless.

'If anybody can hear me please let me know you're there,' I tentatively called out into the blackness.

My voice echoed in the solitude of the space, but no response was heard.

'I apologise for coming into your home uninvited, but the doors were open and I wanted to introduce myself. Can you come towards me and shake my hand to say hello?' I extended my hand into the space before me and waited.

No handshake was forthcoming.

Now at the very highest level of the property, and at the furthest point away from the Chapel – which would act as our base room for the night – I made one last attempt at contact before heading back to meet the other team, who would hopefully now have arrived.

Reaching once again for my mobile phone, I selected a track which seemed to have delivered interesting results on previous investigations at other locations.

The piece, a Gregorian chant called *Te Lucis Ante Terminum*, dates from the 7th century, and the following translation is from the original Latin text.

> To Thee before the close of day,
> Creator of the world, we pray
> That, with Thy wonted favour, Thou
> Wouldst be our guard and keeper now.
>
> From all ill dreams defend our sight,
> From fears and terrors of the night;
> Withhold from us our ghostly foe,
> That spot of sin we may not know.
>
> O Father, that we ask be done,
> Through Jesus Christ, Thine only Son,
> Who, with the Holy Ghost and Thee,
> Doth live and reign eternally.
>
> Amen

Sometimes when trying to gain a person's (or spirit's) attention, we have to push a button. Finding that one thing which they may relate to, or become agitated by, can often be the difference between gaining a result or not.

English history has been heavily divided by religion over the centuries. Henry VIII's break from the Catholic Church, and the subsequent dissolution of the monasteries in the 16th century, led to a huge chasm between Catholics and Protestants for the next two hundred years. Those choosing to observe the 'old faith' were hunted down and persecuted – seen as traitors to the monarch and even sentenced to horrific deaths for treason.

Understanding how divisive this split in religious views may have been to those alive at the time, it makes sense that playing a chant, which has its roots in the Roman Catholic Church, may alienate someone with opposing views, thus making it more likely that they would react and therefore reveal their presence.

In hindsight, choosing to poke the beehive while completely isolated in a dark building, at the top of a spiral staircase, may not have been my smartest move.

Because that's when it happened!

As the final bell tolled to bring the chant to a close, I accepted that nothing would happen and began my descent.

'If you've been trying to reach me then I'd like to thank you,' I began. 'I'm coming back with some friends shortly, so please don't go anywhere as they would love to talk to you.'

I had barely made it down four or five steps – halfway round the first twist of the spiral staircase – when a noise caught my attention.

A small bang, seemingly from somewhere above me in the space I had just left.

There had been no sounds in the five minutes or so that I'd been up there, so this seemed odd. However, with time ticking on and needing to speak with the other team members before the guests began to arrive, I continued downwards, with only the dim light of my torch to safely navigate the perilous stairwell.

And that's when I heard the other sound.

Footsteps!

Slightly on edge from the bang which had just been heard, I'll be honest and say that my heart was now beginning to race a little, and regrets that I now had to make my way through the whole building to reach the sanctuary of the base room began to flood into my mind.

It's quite amazing how quickly the brain can work. In a split second I considered several things.

It's probably just an echo of my footsteps.

I've got a hell of a long walk ahead of me!

Why did I do this?

I paused for the briefest moment, fully expecting the sound of footsteps to stop, and therefore validate my theory of an echo – but they continued.

That's when I picked up my pace. I wasn't going to hang around and find out who, or what, was following me.

But even as I made my way hastily down the remaining stairs, another thought broke into my mind.

I'm on a spiral staircase and can't see what's behind me or in front of me. Are those sounds coming from above, or am I heading straight towards them?

I've never been truly terrified by anything while doing this job, even though I've had some hair-raising moments, but this is probably the closest I've come to genuine fear, and isn't a feeling I'd ever like to experience again.

As I reached the relative safety of the base room I was glad to be greeted by one of the Haunted Happenings team, along with two staff members from the Towers who had come to set up the refreshments for the night ahead.

For my own sanity I had to be sure none of them had come into the building. I needed to know if they could possibly have been responsible for the bang, or the footsteps I believed I'd heard.

They hadn't.

They vouched for each other that they'd all been in the Chapel for the five minutes before I'd appeared, and had assumed I had been over to the toilet block rather than being in the building alone.

Who would be crazy enough to do that?

The footsteps at Alton Towers left a lasting impression upon me. I could find no rational explanation for the sounds I heard up there, and the building went on to deliver some other frights that night for the guests who took part in the subsequent ghost hunt.

Did the religious chant annoy somebody up there? Did I allow my imagination to run away with me?

On the drive home in the early hours of the following morning, while considering the whole episode, something hit me like a truck.

I was wearing trainers!

The footsteps had been a hollow clunking sound on the stone, yet my footwear made no sound whatsoever.

I was right after all.

It wasn't me!

(Above) The 'whispering hallway' at The Station Hotel in Dudley.

The infamous room 214 is pictured above (first room on the right up the steps). This photograph was taken beside room 216, outside which a whispering voice was heard during the night of 21 September 2013. No explanation was found.

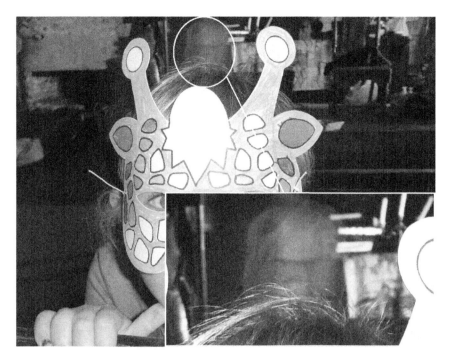

(Above) The photograph taken in the undercroft at Dudley Castle on 6 June 2010 during a children's birthday party. In the background appears to be the figure of a woman in white. The image remains unexplained.

(Below) The same area of the undercroft, showing the platform and suit of armour

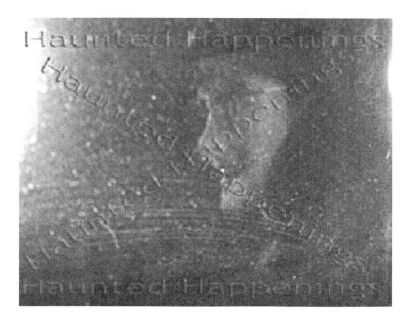

(Above) The 'airman in the attic' photograph, captured at Woodchester Mansion in Gloucestershire on 27 March 2010 during a ghost hunting event with Haunted Happenings – (Image courtesy of Haunted Happenings)

(Below) Bran Castle – Dracula's Castle – in Transylvania, Romania. The building houses a display of medieval torture equipment and sits atop a secret tunnel.

(Above) The execution room at The Dana Prison (Shrewsbury). It was on the exact spot where the mannequin is standing that the EVP of what sounds like a man's voice whispering the words "don't tempt me" was captured on 27 August 2016.

(Above) The state apartments of Warwick Castle, outside which the shadowy figure was seen

(Below) The Kenilworth bedroom in which Daisy (Countess of Warwick) allegedly conducted séances during the late-19th century, joined by the notorious Aleister Crowley. It is said that an abandoned séance resulted in an entity being released that still haunts the castle today.

(Above) An 'extra guest' was captured during a group photograph at Newsham Park Hospital on 31 October 2016. Nobody knew who the person was or recognised them from the event. (Image courtesy of Haunted Happenings)

(Below) The Hallway of 30 East Drive in Pontefract, where a ghostly monk allegedly terrorised the Pritchard family in 1966. (Image courtesy of Haunted Happenings)

7

NEWSHAM PARK HOSPITAL
Liverpool - Merseyside

Every once in a while a new location comes onto the radar; something which is special – an instant hit with ghost hunters, and a place which quickly gains (and earns) itself a reputation for quite extreme paranormal activity.

Newsham Park Hospital is one of those places!

Since the first ghost hunt took place inside its walls in May 2013, literally thousands of eager paranormal enthusiasts have crossed the threshold in search of a ghostly encounter.

Like most who have been there, I'll never forget my first visit to the abandoned hospital.

It was a cold spring-morning in early March. The bare branches of trees lined the approach to the hospital, along the aptly named Orphan Drive, and morning birdsong carried effortlessly through the still air.

Daffodils scattered the grass verges of the lake in the centre of Newsham Park, and as I gazed up at the vast and imposing building before me, the thick mist of my breath hung as heavy as a dense fog.

The place was staggering!

As I gazed in awe at the imposing Victorian institution before me, I wondered to myself whether the barbed-wire which adorned the perimeter fencing had been added to keep unwanted visitors out – or to keep the patients in.

I made my way cautiously through the rusted wrought-iron gates and into the compound, taking care to avoid the overgrown brambles, their gnarly branches reaching forth as if attempting to wrap themselves around me; stretching arms trying to devour any new life which entered.

Inside, daylight broke through the cracks of boarded windows, casting much-needed shards of light upon darkened rooms, and breathing life into the now desolate space.

Cracked paint peeled from every wall, and the cubicles in the wards – once a place of rest and recuperation – now stood empty, with privacy curtains hanging lifelessly from the rails.

Down in the basement the empty lockers which had once served the hospital's staff still contained a few items – left behind some sixteen years previously – including a single shoe and a roll-on deodorant stick.

Throughout the building a number of wheelchairs stood, like broken-down vehicles, abandoned on the spot where they had delivered their last useful means of transport many years before.

I had been invited to visit the building to assess whether it would be a viable location for ghost hunting groups, and it was immediately obvious that – even though there was no real knowledge of any paranormal activity at this point – it would be the ideal place to investigate.

So much history. So much pain and suffering. So many rooms to explore.

It had everything!

The building began its life in 1879, as an orphanage for children whose parents had been lost at sea, becoming home to over 1,000 children by the time the great-war ended in 1918.

With new laws which prohibited young children living in an institutional-school, and great expansion of the country's social-services schemes, the Orphanage closed in 1949, making way for a new hospital whose doors opened in 1954.

The hospital had officially stopped taking new patients by 1988, and by 1992 all patients and staff had been relocated. However, with the closure of the nearby Rainhill Lunatic Asylum, the inmates were moved to Newsham Park Hospital – taking up to 90% of its space – and around £1.6m was spent on making the facilities suitable for its new patients.

It seemed logical to me that the angst and suffering which had been endured over the years inside this place must have left a mark; an indelible stain upon the fabric of the building, which not even the passing of years would erase.

If the stone tape theory is true – a belief that buildings absorb people's emotions and energy and release it in years to come – then surely a place where children were treated harshly, and psychiatric patients subjected to electroconvulsive therapy, would be the ideal conduit.

It didn't take long to find out that those initial instincts and beliefs were right. In less than six months the abandoned hospital had secured its place as the UK's number one ghost hunting location, and delivered a number of terrifying encounters for those brave enough to see it for themselves.

An Unexpected Guest

In November 2016 Haunted Happenings and Newsham Park Hospital hit the national headlines after a rather alarming picture was taken on the night of 31 October – Halloween.

"Zombie-like phantom photobombs visitor tour at an old orphanage in an image so eerie even the ghost hunters say they're spooked." – Daily Mail Online (7 November 2016)

At the beginning of every Haunted Happenings ghost hunt the team take a photograph of the group, which is then uploaded to the company's Facebook page the following day, so that guests can leave comments about their experiences and keep it as a memento of the event.

On this particular night three guests were late to arrive and the photograph was taken without them, in order to get the ghost hunting underway.

The picture was taken on the host's mobile phone and – after lightening the image slightly – it was emailed immediately to the company's offices to be uploaded onto the social media page.

At the time nobody noticed anything unusual, and it wasn't until the following day that visitors to the page began to comment upon one particular face in the picture; the image of a woman which looked somehow out of place.

Right there, in the very centre of the group, a woman's face. Her features are considerably paler than those of the guests around her.

The "corpse-like figure" began to attract a lot of attention on social media, leading to much speculation about whether a ghost had really been captured on camera, or if she was actually just one of the guests taking part in the event.

In order to clarify this point and ensure it wasn't simply a case of mistaken identity, the company e-mailed each and every guest who booked places on the event in an attempt to discover if anyone recognised the person as one of their group.

Nobody recognised the face.

In fact, nobody present on the night even remembered anybody in the group resembling this person.

In a subsequent interview, the founder of Haunted Happenings, Hazel Ford, commented that the size of the face seemed out of proportion with everyone else's in the picture.

To this day the image remains a mystery.

But this isn't the first time unexplained images have been captured at Newsham Park Hospital.

During an earlier investigation a ghost hunter captured a similarly startling image – what appears to be a face looking through the glass panel of a door, leading from Ward G on the ground floor, into the day room.

Although not as clear as the one taken on Halloween night in 2016, the face in this image appears to be looking towards the person taking the photograph, standing approximately twenty feet away from the doorway.

In both cases nobody saw anything out of the ordinary at the time the photographs were taken, but later spotted the anomalies while reviewing them.

Nobody at Haunted Happenings has ever claimed either of these images are definitely something paranormal. In fact, they are always very clear about making the point that we just don't know for sure.

So are we just making things fit to satisfy our minds that ghosts really do exist?

Perhaps!

In 1977 the image of Jesus Christ appeared on a flour tortilla, in a small town forty minutes south of Roswell in the USA. In 2004 a ten-year-old grilled-cheese sandwich sold on e-bay for $28,000, with claims that it bore the image of Jesus. A staggering number of people even believed that an image taken of Mars in 1976 showed a face on the planet's surface – asserting that this was "proof" of Martian civilization.

Of course all of these 'sightings' are almost certainly nonsense, but they're all great examples of Pareidolia – a psychological phenomenon in which the mind creates images by perceiving patterns which are familiar to us, where no actual pattern exists.

As human beings our minds are pre-programmed to make sense of random shapes and images.

The complexities of the brain are barely understood, even today, but what we do know is that it is not uncommon for people to 'see' faces and shapes in all sorts of unusual places.

Rock formations can create recognisable forms through weathering and erosion, so it's quite understandable that people will often believe that they can see faces within the stonework of a building.

So if you add this phenomena into the context of a ghost hunt – where those taking part are already predisposed to *want* to see something – it is easy to see how these images can come about in the minds of those seeking proof of the paranormal.

Sceptics will always be quick to label images reporting to reveal ghostly shapes as examples of Pareidolia, or worse, clever Photoshop editing.

With huge advances in photo editing software in the last twenty years, it has become much easier for anyone with a reasonable level of skill to generate a 'ghost photo', and much harder for anyone to prove it as a fake.

The sad irony of this is, without advances in technology, we will probably never really gain irrefutable proof that ghosts exist. However, I believe that it may also be those very same technological advances which prevent it happening.

This could well become one of the greatest, and saddest, contradictions mankind will endure.

Turn out the Lights

Basements, cellars and attics. Why is it that these are always the places we expect to encounter ghostly activity? Is it because they are often the darkest and most spooky looking areas of a building? Could it be that we assume spirits will lurk in these places in an attempt to stay away from the living? Is it because those are the rooms where the worst paranormal experiences happen in Hollywood movies?

Whatever the reason, these are often the places a ghost hunter will relish. Those areas most are drawn to in search of the paranormal.

At Newsham Park Hospital visitors are blessed with a vast location to explore, from psychiatric wards, where patients were once heavily sedated and 'experimented' on, to dark corridors, where naughty children were allegedly locked into small cupboards as punishment for misbehaviour during the building's time as an orphanage.

With so many spaces to investigate, why is it that the laundry basement has become one of the most feared to venture into alone?

The answer is simple; past experiences in this area have frightened and amazed in equal measure, and it's those moments we all seek when reaching out to the spirit world.

It is those which send adrenaline coursing through our veins, and make the heart beat so fast that you feel it could burst right from your chest.

The basement is accessed by a single wood-panelled doorway. A twisting stone staircase leads down into the darkness, paint flaking from the walls, long since giving up hope of ever being restored.

A lengthy corridor, with no natural light, leads to a number of open doorways into smaller side rooms, where empty lockers stand in rows like soldiers, and laundry equipment – archaic by today's standards – now lies redundant.

People have often reported inexplicable sensations of unease when entering these spaces, with one man even describing feeling an invisible force – like a surge of electricity – pass through his whole body.

But it was a simple torch which caused great alarm on one particular night, during a watch and wait vigil with a small group at the beginning of an event.

The ghost hunt was barely underway when it happened. A group of around fifteen people had made their way into the basement to view the space, and carry out a short vigil. Two guests had positioned themselves at either end of the corridor, to report back on any noises or temperature changes. The remainder of the group created a circle mid-way down the corridor, and linked hands while calling forward any spirits which may have been present.

'Can you please give us a sign that you are here with us?' one of the investigators called out into the blackness.

A hushed silence followed, each of the participants listening intently for the slightest sound to indicate a response.

But nothing came.

'Please could you step close to one of us and see if you can make yourself known?'

Nothing was reported by the group, although one of the EMF meters did begin to register an increase of energy.

Then it happened.

A dull glow of light suddenly appeared on the outskirts of the circle, drawing the attention of everyone in the group.

'What's that light over there?' someone asked.

'I can see it too,' came another voice, then another, and another.

The blanket of blackness to which everyone's eyes had become accustomed had been partially lifted, the glow from whatever it was offering some respite from the darkness.

'Can everyone please remain exactly as you are?' the host leading the vigil requested. 'I'm going to turn on my light and see if we can work out what it is?'

The host released the hands of those either side and reached for his torch. The strange glow, so obvious to everyone in the room, must have been coming from a man-made source, but without exploring that they would not be able to debunk it;

hence the reason for switching on another torch.

As the room lit further the source of the light became immediately obvious.

'Ah, I can see what it is.' the host began. Pointing towards one lady in the group, he went on to reveal that her torch had switched on while in her pocket.

'It seemed too good to be true, but at least we know now,' he went on. 'Could you just make sure it's fully twisted to the off position for me please?' he asked the lady.

But she looked puzzled.

'It's a push button torch and I've been holding hands with these ladies either side of me the whole time.' she explained.

How the hell can that happen?

One of the difficulties of taking part in a public ghost hunting event is that you can never been certain of everyone's intentions, and there is always a possibility that somebody could be in attendance who isn't taking things as seriously as the majority.

It is an unfortunate reality of life, but one that the hosts are very aware of, and will always do their level best to prevent happening.

Nobody should go in search of a paranormal experience and leave questioning if something had been faked. Trust is paramount, and as hosts we will do everything within our power to ensure that nobody fakes activity within the course of the event.

It was important to establish quickly if the people the lady was holding hands with were friends or relatives, to eliminate the possibility that they had released hands to allow her to press the button and then pretend otherwise.

They were not related.

In fact, the people standing each side of the lady whose torch had illuminated were not even in the same booking group.

Both insisted that their hands had remained connected

throughout, and that the lady hadn't moved just prior to the light coming on.

Looks of amazement and bewilderment filled the space.

'Okay,' the host began. 'If you could switch it off again for us please and leave it in your pocket, we will see if it happens again.'

Everyone in the circle re-linked their hands and the room was returned to darkness.

'If there's somebody in the room with us who approached the lady and created that light, could you please do it again to show us it wasn't an accident?'

The group waited, barely a breath could be heard as the anticipation rose.

'There it is again,' someone exclaimed, as the room once again glowed through the fabric of the lady's jacket pocket.

Okay – if they're somehow hoaxing us in the dark then I've got an idea.

'Thank you, whoever that was,' the host began. 'We'd like to continue talking with you if you don't mind, but only with the lights off. So would you mind making the room dark again for us please?

Still dubious about the authenticity of the 'activity' which had just been experienced, the host wanted to see the light switch back off.

Of course, with the glow from the lady's pocket it was now possible for the group to make out her figure, and those either side of her too, so even if they had been messing around while it was dark, there was no possible way that they could do it now that they could be seen.

Then it happened.

The light was extinguished, and a gasp of nervous excitement swept through the group, like a high-speed train whooshing through a station.

Further examination of the torch, after the vigil had ended, revealed that the button needed to switch it on was sturdy, and highly unlikely that it could possibly switch on just from a small movement of the body.

The batteries were checked to eliminate the possibility they were low on charge, and the switch appeared to be working properly, because when it was checked back in the base room it remained on when switched on, and off when turned off.

It would seem that the ghostly light-show experienced in the basements had no obvious explanation, leaving just one possibility.

"When you have eliminated the impossible, whatever remains, however improbable, must be the truth" – Arthur Conan Doyle

8

THE SKIRRID MOUNTAIN INN
Abergavenny – South Wales

At the easternmost outline of the Black Mountains in Wales lies the Skirrid; a distinctively shaped, red-sandstone hill, reaching 486m high at its peak.

The name comes from the Welsh word for shiver, 'Ysgyryd', and legend has it that over two thousand years ago – in the hours after the crucifixion of Christ – part of the mountain literally broke away. Many believed that the earth from the hill was especially fertile, even holy, and it was common for soil to be removed and scattered in the foundations of nearby churches.

The mystical Skirrid is shrouded in rich a mythology, and high upon the summit the ruins of an iron-age hill fort and medieval chapel can still be seen today.

Rock tables, formed by centuries-old landslides, have created a distinctive stone which – for reasons unknown – has been labelled 'The Devil's Table'.

In the shadows of the hill, in the small village of Llanvihangel

Crucorney, sits what is reported to be the oldest pub in Wales – the Skirrid Mountain Inn.

Said to date back almost 1100 years, the Inn is home to many popular legends of its own.

One such story is that Owain Glyndŵr rallied supporters of the Welsh revolt from the cobbles of the inn's courtyard in the 15th century, before raiding settlements which sympathised with the English king, Henry VI.

On a more macabre level, the upper floor of the inn is also said to have been used as a courtroom, where sentences were handed down – and allegedly carried out – for crimes such as sheep stealing and other petty offences.

Although there is little documented evidence to support this – and the actual date of establishment for the existing building is thought to be from the 17th century – it has been said that as many as 180 souls were lost on the premises, sentenced to hang for their crimes.

It is claimed that markings in the wood of the staircase serve as a reminder of where the rope carried out its grim obligations in the name of justice.

Whether or not these stories are true is perhaps less relevant than the reports of paranormal activity which have been made over a number of years.

When a former landlady of the inn decided to sell it, glasses were allegedly thrown by an unseen force across the kitchen.

Other phenomena has been cited which includes the sound of a lady's dress rustling, and the sweet, powerful scent of perfume wafting through certain rooms.

Fanny Price worked at the inn during the 18th century. She lived to the age of just thirty-five before succumbing to the terrible disease consumption, and her body is now buried – alongside other members of her family – in the local parish churchyard, just a few hundred yards up the road from the Skirrid Inn.

Local legend has it that Fanny still roams the inn to this day, and it is thought by many that it is she who is responsible for much of the activity experienced there – especially in the area around and behind the bar.

Whether she is accountable for those experiences in the inn or not, there are plenty who would testify to some thoroughly inexplicable events within its centuries old walls. And it would seem it's not just spirits of the inn itself which would like to make themselves known.

Knock Knock, Who's there?

One dark November night, a small group of guests made their way to the churchyard in search of the Price family graves, to see for themselves the final resting place of the now infamous Fanny.

Of course, out of respect for those who now rest in this pretty churchyard – and their families – nobody had any intention of carrying out a ghost hunt.

But with a night of paranormal investigation ahead of them at the inn – and a belly full of chocolate fudge cake to walk off – it seemed a fitting time to make a visit and take a look at the church itself.

The temperature was particularly cold that night. An icy breeze nipped at exposed hands and faces, biting and unwelcoming.

Tiny clusters of light scattered the cloudless skies, billions of stars watching over the group as they made their way through the wrought iron gates, past the many gravestones which scatter the land surrounding the church.

To shelter from the bitter breeze, the group huddled together in the small shelter which leads into the church, while the hosts explained a little of the background to the inn, and the whereabouts of Fanny's grave.

It was during this brief exchange, when one of the guests asked a question about ghosts and spirits, that something unexpected happened.

Thud, thud.

Suddenly, and without any request, two unmistakable bangs were heard by the door leading into the property. Two clear knocks, seemingly from the heavy wooden door itself.

People's faces were a mix of shock and fear. Nobody had expected it, and naturally the group was intrigued.

'Is there somebody inside the church?' someone asked.

'There certainly shouldn't be,' the host responded, 'and there's no sign of any lights on inside.'

The person closest to the door tried the handle to see if it was indeed still open.

It was locked – as expected.

One of the Haunted Happenings team stepped towards the doorway, knocked back, and shouted 'hello?'

There was no response.

Once again the host knocked, placing an ear carefully to the door in an attempt to hear if anybody were inside.

But once again, nothing came.

Interestingly, when the group knocked from the outside the sound was different. Everyone present who heard the sounds was convinced that they had come from the other side of the doorway; somebody or something trying to get their attention from inside the locked church.

With no further responses to their knocks, and with a full night of ghost hunting beckoning, the group sheepishly made their way back towards the Skirrid Inn, puzzled and in shock at what had just occurred at St Michael's parish church.

It is unknown whether this had ever happened before, or since, and it would be impossible to say with absolute certainty that the group didn't fall foul of a prank by a mischievous vicar.

But I guess that's all part of the fun of ghost hunting; those unexpected moments when something happens which leaves you scratching your head in search of answers.

The Wardrobe in Room 2

True poltergeist activity is a rarity. To witness an object move of its own accord, by unseen hands, is an experience which would surely terrify even the most hardened ghost hunter or sceptic.

So, it was of little surprise that a group of four people fled room 2 – in a barrage of screams and panic – when they encountered something in the darkened bedroom.

A force so strong that, no matter how hard they tried to find a rational explanation, they could not recreate what had happened.

Room 2, on the upper floor of the Skirrid Inn, is full of character. A stunning four-poster bed lies majestically to the right as you enter the room, and a small sofa sits in the centre of the room, facing a period dressing table upon which a modern, flat-screen television is perched.

Directly ahead of you as you enter the room – behind and to the left of the sofa – is a large, freestanding wardrobe, fashioned from a dark wood to fit aesthetically with the other furniture in the room.

In the moments leading up to the activity, the group of four – three ladies and one gentleman – had been sitting in darkness, trying to make contact with any of the spirits who might reside there.

With a number of pieces of paranormal detection devices, including a K2 meter – designed to alert users to any spikes in EMF energy – they requested that anyone present in the room with them come forward and make themselves known.

With no sign of any activity to prepare them for what was about to happen, the man began to move around the back of the sofa with the K2 meter, in an attempt to seek out any shift in the energy of the room.

After taking just a few steps towards the bed, the silence was suddenly broken by a loud crash.

In the panic of the moment everyone reached for their torches, assuming that someone had knocked something over in the room.

But what they were confronted with was far more frightening than they expected.

When they had begun the vigil, a small folding luggage rack had been leaning against the doors of the wardrobe.

Now, some distance away from the nearest person in the room, the wardrobe door was wide open, and the luggage rack lay on its side – several feet away from it.

The realisation of what had happened dawned in an instant, and fear crashed down upon them like a huge breaking wave.

All four of the group fled the room in sheer panic, tumbling one after the other down the staircase and into the bar, where the hosts were seated.

Reluctantly, the group agreed to return to the room with the hosts to investigate the aftermath of the incident, and seek an explanation for what had happened.

It's all too easy to jump to conclusions when something unexpected occurs during a ghost hunt, and to perceive things as paranormal where there may be a quite simple and rational commentary.

Darkened rooms, stories of hauntings and ancient buildings are the perfect mix to generate fear, and of course our minds are capable of creating all sorts of scenarios if we allow them to, whilst overlooking the obvious.

But on this occasion there was no 'obvious' to be found.

The most plausible possibility was that an uneven floorboard had dislodged the door of the wardrobe when the gentleman in the group walked across the room, somehow causing it to spring open and push the luggage rack to the floor.

So, it was time to recreate that very scenario.

When they settled down to conduct the vigil, two were seated on the end of the four-poster bed, and the others had been seated on the sofa, until the man stood up to walk behind it.

With the door secured and the luggage rack back in place, they set about re-tracing the steps he had taken just before it happened.

It had no effect. The doors didn't budge.

The gentleman also pointed out that when they first entered the room they had all walked around in different places, before settling down into their positions. The wardrobe doors had remained firmly closed throughout this, and showed no signs of moving.

With the doors refusing to budge from the movement of the floorboards, they decided to test how far the luggage rack would be moved if they pulled the doors open by hand.

It had travelled around four feet from the wardrobe when the incident occurred earlier, so they expected – with a swift pull on the wardrobe door – that it would fall in a similar place now.

It didn't.

Even after three attempts, pulling the door open with some force, the luggage rack failed to reach anywhere near the same distance it had before.

Whatever had caused the wardrobe door to swing open had also managed to propel the luggage rack further than we could with our own hands.

Was this a genuine display of poltergeist activity at the Skirrid Inn? Did this group of eager ghost hunters really experience the true force of an entity within room 2 of this centuries old pub? Was this a one-off occurrence?

We will never know the answers to the first two questions. However, when discussing this incident with another of the company's hosts several weeks later, the host that night was shocked and amazed to learn that the door to this wardrobe – in the very same room – had opened itself during a completely different investigation some months earlier.

Except there was one significant difference.

On that occasion the door hadn't swung open with any force. In the blackness during a watch & wait vigil – with nobody walking around in the room – the door had opened gently of its own accord.

The eerie creaking sound of it opening had been heard by the whole group, with nobody nearby, and when they turned on the lights to see what the sound was, one of the doors was ajar; open by around eight inches.

If you're planning to book an overnight stay at the Skirrid Inn then beware. You may wake in the morning to find your clothes are missing!

9

THE OLD WORKHOUSE
Leeds – West Yorkshire

In this modern age it is difficult for many of us to understand the harsh life that some our ancestors once endured.

The most familiar images presented to us in paintings and photographs of Victorian life are bleak. Blankets of smog loom over industrialised towns and cities, violent criminals lurk in the shadows of overcrowded streets, and impoverished children work in atrocious conditions.

In Victorian England there was a distinct divide between the conditions lived by the rich and those of their poorer counterparts.

Wealthy Victorians enjoyed a relatively easy life. Usually well fed and clothed, the elite of society often lived in big houses with their own servants. Their children had expensive toys to play with and received an education, and the family would enjoy holidays in much the same way that the majority of us do today.

In contrast, the poor of society had few, if any, luxuries in life. The food they ate was often of poor quality and scant in quantity. Filthy, damp living conditions were the cause of great disease and high rates of infant mortality.

Most of the children from poorer families would be forced to work from a young age instead of attending school, making it difficult to ever make the transition from poor to rich.

For the working poor life was also dangerous.

In Scotland the infamous Burke & Hare preyed on the unfortunate souls who lived in the city of Edinburgh's slums, killing sixteen people in a period of around ten months in 1828.

For the 'working girls' of London, the need to find a means of earning money outweighed the risk of falling victim to the elusive serial-killer Jack the Ripper.

Even the children of poor families had dangers to endure, for many would be sent to work in the mills and mines which now supported the rise of the industrial age – clambering under and around heavy machinery from as young as five years of age.

A great chasm divided the two social groups and, for anyone who fell into the poor category, there was an even greater fear than that which they already suffered.

The threat of the workhouse!

The New Poor Law of 1834 aimed to reduce spending on welfare for the poor. Those who found themselves unable to sustain a living sufficient for their families were sent to the new workhouses, where families were split up.

Those who were able to work were forced into hard labour in return for a roof over their head, and those who couldn't were cared for at the most basic standard.

Either way the conditions were harsh, and treatment was often cruel.

Conditions in the workhouses were often horrifying, with some even resorting to criminal offences in order to be given a custodial sentence, as both the accommodation and food were considered better in prison.

For those already living on the bread-line, the threat of the workhouse loomed heavily, for they were only an accident away from not being able to provide for themselves. A simple broken leg or an illness could result in the need for support, and see the whole family sent to the workhouse.

In 2012 I visited what was once the Leeds Union Workhouse building – now home to the Thackray Medical Museum – to meet with the staff and discuss the possibility of organising public ghost hunts there.

The weather conditions were terrible that evening, with heavy snow beginning to fall by the time we arrived.

As well as its time as a workhouse – housing up to 784 of the poorest folk of Leeds – the building had also served as a hospital during the First World War.

It now offers visitors the opportunity to wander down a replica Victorian-slum street, and view surgical equipment from across the ages, including Prince Albert's personal medical chest.

At the time of this visit, the skeletal remains of the infamous Mary Bateman were on display. Bateman was a criminal and alleged witch – known at the Yorkshire Witch – who was tried and executed for murder during the early 19th century.

With so much torment and history, how could this building not be haunted?

However, with only a short tour planned before heading off to the nearby Armley Mills for an overnight ghost hunt, none of us expected to encounter anything paranormal at the time.

How wrong we were!

The Missing Footprints

We had arrived at the old workhouse at around 5.30pm. The vast Victorian façade loomed ominously, with only a few lights visible in some of the large windows to signify any life inside whatsoever.

Our guides, two staff members of the museum, were on hand

to show us around the building and share with us some of the history and ghostly experiences they themselves have witnessed.

The building is vast. A grand staircase leads to a gallery landing from the main entrance hallway, and a series of rooms lead from one to the next, each with its own theme.

The tour ended on the ground floor, in a room overlooking the carpark at the front of the property.

The snow had settled fast and there was little light outside from the moon that night to illuminate the exterior; the yellowish glow of street lights providing little respite from the dark winter night.

While in conversation with our guides, somebody passed by the window; a shadow in the darkness, passing from right to left – walking in the direction of the main entrance.

At the time none of us visiting thought anything of it, assuming it was just a member of the public walking past the museum, en route to wherever they were heading.

However, the staff from the building looked puzzled.

'What's up?' I asked.

'I'm just wondering what that person is doing in the grounds at this time of night,' our guide responded. She looked genuinely concerned that somebody would be approaching the museum at this hour.

She approached the window in an attempt to see where the person was going, but the angle prevented us seeing anything further than a few meters in the direction they had been walking. While standing at the window, searching for the mystery person, something occurred to me.

There were no footprints in the snow.

How can somebody have just walked past and not left a mark on the ground?

I pointed this out to them and they looked equally bemused.

There were five people in that room that evening, and every one of us saw somebody walk past the window. Now, just a few seconds later, the snow lay entirely undisturbed on the ground, revealing no clues as to where the mysterious figure had gone.

Moments like these are rare. Or perhaps they're not.

I once worked with a psychic medium who made a very valid point about ghost sightings.

As we go about our day-to-day lives – the commute to work or maybe a trip to the shopping centre – we encounter literally hundreds of people. Regular looking folk who we assume are just as alive as we ourselves are, but we never actually come into contact with the vast majority of them.

Could it be at all possible that one or more of those whose paths we cross are actually ghostly figures, also going about their business?

However unlikely this seems, it is possible.

Perhaps we all see ghosts and just never realise it.

Anything is possible.

-10-

30 EAST DRIVE
Pontefract – West Yorkshire

In 1977 the national headlines were ablaze with sensational coverage of an alleged poltergeist haunting in a suburban council house in Enfield, near London.

In August of that year, single parent Peggy Hodgson telephoned the police and reported that two of her children had been terrified when they witnessed furniture moving in the house of its own accord, and heard knocking sounds coming from within the walls.

When the police attended, a female constable testified that she witnessed a chair move with nobody nearby, and what resulted was one of the most carefully documented 'hauntings' of our time.

But they were not the first family to suffer such an ordeal, because some 180 miles north – in the summer of 1966 – the Pritchard family had experienced similar events, in their semi-detached house on East Drive, Pontefract.

Married couple Jean and Joe Pritchard moved into their new

home on East Drive in August 1966, along with their two children, Phillip, aged 15, and Diane, aged 12.

Almost immediately after settling into the house, the family began to notice strange things were happening. Fine chalk was seen falling from mid-air, and mysterious pools of water appeared from nowhere on the linoleum flooring in the kitchen.

What began as a few unexplained oddities soon escalated to several years of terrifying, inexplicable events.

Lights would switch on and off, cupboard doors would shake violently, furniture within the house reportedly levitated, and – even more alarmingly – photographs were slashed by a sharp knife.

The events, as if not frightening enough already, culminated in a physical attack upon Diane, and the whole family were allegedly witness to the extreme actions, believed to have been caused by a malevolent poltergeist.

The Black Monk

Jean refused to be forced from her home by this unknown entity and, probably in an attempt to normalise the unwelcome visitor who was wreaking havoc on the home, the family decided to name it Fred.

Poor Diane seemed to be the focus of much of the poltergeist's attention, although it was Jean and Joe who first witnessed the manifestation – a mysterious, black-robed figure, floating over their bed one night.

The couple described the vision as resembling that of a Monk, due to the robes it wore.

One paranormal investigator, who spent years researching the haunting of 30 East Drive, reported that the town's gallows had been situated just across the street from where the Pritchard's house now stood.

Folklore tells of a Clunaic monk who was sentenced to hang at those very gallows for the rape and murder of a young girl, and it has been suggested that this was the character now responsible for the ordeal suffered by the Pritchard family.

At the height of the Pontefract haunting Diane was said to have been dragged kicking and screaming up the stairs by an invisible force, an event which left her utterly traumatised and with clearly visible finger marks around her throat.

Was this really the work of a murderous Black Monk of Pontefract?

Did the family invent the story for publicity?

Is the house really haunted?

They are all valid questions.

The haunting eventually ceased, and the house remained in the ownership of the Pritchard family until May 2012, when it was purchased by a private owner.

But it wasn't the end!

In that same year, a film director by the name of Pat Holden decided he wanted to immortalise the haunting of 30 East Drive. Holden was Jean Pritchard's nephew and had apparently witnessed some of the incidents at the house first hand.

The family weren't keen when approached to discuss the events, and were fearful that the film might anger the spirits once more, leading to further problems. Holden went ahead with the movie, but filming took place at a Huddersfield studio instead of the property itself.

When the Lights Went Out tells the story of the Pritchard's terror at the hands of a poltergeist. Much of the film's narrative is based on the real-life incidents which took place during that summer, although the family's names were changed.

The new owner – the producer of the movie – couldn't resist purchasing the property when he discovered it was up for sale.

At the time of the film's release, the Pritchard's next door neighbour gave an interview with the Daily Star Online, in which she described the moment she found out that the house had been sold.

She had noticed Phillip Pritchard outside the house one afternoon, tidying up the garden. She'd made the assumption that Phillip had sold the property to a nephew, who she knew to be hard of hearing, having become aware of the television blasting out through the adjoining wall late into the night.

But the house was empty; there was no television inside and nobody had moved in.

Phillip allegedly turned pale when she informed him of this and said, 'God, it's started again.'

She has not seen him since!

30 East Drive has since been opened to the public for overnight paranormal investigations and ghost hunting events, and based on the experiences described by those who have spent the night there, it would appear that the spirits are very much still present.

In recent years several photographs have been shared by investigators who have spent time in the property.

On more than one occasion, a black mass has been captured on camera in the hallway leading to the first floor. One of those pictures appears to show a hand reaching out from behind the bannister, and in another – taken of the hallway – what looks like a face is visible in the reflection of the mirror which hangs at the bottom of the stairs.

It is worthy of note that these pictures all seem to have captured something unusual in the same area of the property that poor Diane suffered her final ordeal at the hands of the entity.

None of the photographs have been examined and verified as authentic, so it is up to the individual to make of them what they will, but it's not just the pictures which have captured the attention of ghost hunters.

The list of strange encounters and unusual experiences within 30 East Drive continues to grow.

Hell Hath no Fury

On the evening of 18 March 2017, one of the Haunted Happenings hosts arrived to unlock the house ahead of a night of ghost hunting.

Joined by one other team member, the pair had arrived with sufficient time to set up the tea & coffee station before the guests were expected.

Having led many ghost hunts at the property before, they unloaded the car and prepared some equipment for the guests to use later, before heading upstairs to check that all was in order with the rest of the house.

Whilst upstairs the pair became aware of banging noises which seemed to come from within the house. Several dull thuds were heard in the space of just a few seconds; then there was something else.

Whilst crossing the landing they were stopped in their tracks by another sound – different this time.

'Did you hear that?' the host asked.

'Keys?'

'Yeah.'

The remained still for a few seconds, listening intently. Eyes darting from one corner of the landing to the other, their bodies tensed in anticipation of what might follow.

'You've not got anything on you that jangles have you?' the host whispered.

'Nope. I left everything downstairs.'

The pair crept silently down the stairs and along the hallway, peering around the doorframe into the lounge as they went.

Nothing.

It wouldn't be long before the first guests would arrive, so, feeling a little unnerved by the noises they'd just been hearing, they decided to step outside for a few minutes – and that's when they noticed something was missing.

The keys to the front door were gone!

"I've heard stories of the poltergeist's obsession with keys, and until tonight I've never experienced this. I tell u what, he's met his match tonight. Hell hath no fury like a woman who's spent 20 minutes looking for her keys - eventually found hidden in the kitchen."

This Facebook comment, uploaded by the host later that night, attracted several comments over the following days, many of which were from others who had spent the night investigating 30 East Drive for themselves – sharing their own experiences of this spooky suburban semi.

Human beings are terrible at losing things when they're busy. Stories of the TV remote ending up in the refrigerator are pretty common, while looking for your spectacles when you're already wearing them is another popular calamity many have befallen. Basically, as a species we're easily distracted and often misplace things.

However, we are also creatures of habit; especially where common and repetitive jobs are concerned. Having carried out many, many investigations of 30 East Drive, the host had a fairly robust routine.

Arrive. Unlock the house. Carry all the equipment and refreshments from the car into the kitchen. Throw keys and bags onto the kitchen work surface. Make an inspection of the house before the guests arrive, etc.

The house keys are never left in the door on arrival, so they'd been placed on the kitchen worktop which is on the right as you enter the room.

Although circumstances sometimes necessitate a change in the routine, everything had gone exactly as planned that night; until they returned to the kitchen and made the discovery.

The search began!

Pockets were checked, bags were emptied, and their steps

through the house retraced in an attempt to find the missing keys.

They were nowhere to be seen.

Panic began to set in. The pair considered that perhaps they'd actually forgotten to lock the front door, and that somebody must have entered the house and stolen them.

But nothing else has been taken!

A nervous look through the kitchen window revealed that the car was still parked outside. A check of the front door also confirmed that it was still locked.

Has somebody actually taken the keys and locked us in?

There were no signs that anybody had been in the house. Nothing was missing. Nothing was out of place, yet the keys were not where they had been left just a short while earlier.

They turned the house upside down. The guests would soon arrive, and the only set of keys in their possession were still nowhere to be found.

Every conceivable place was searched. Kitchen drawers were opened, both handbags were turned out onto the table, and every work surface re-checked in desperation.

They were eventually found in the most unexpected of places; on the floor *behind* the cooker.

What the hell are they doing there?

The keys were quickly retrieved – using a dowsing rod as a hook – and they were finally ready to welcome the guests.

As with any incidents of potential paranormal activity, the rational mind begins to cast doubt upon a situation.

People often blame each other for playing pranks. Suspicion of foul play by human hands always lurks in the back of the mind – a natural assumption which helps our logical minds make sense of illogical situations. We doubt ourselves and consider that perhaps we have either forgotten doing something, or worse, we doubt our own judgement.

But the pair had remained together since entering the house, neither leaving the other's side before heading upstairs.

And what of the sound of keys jangling they believed they had heard earlier? Could that have been when they were moved?

Poltergeist activity is rarely physical towards people, or aimed at causing intentional harm.

In most of the documented cases the entity seems more interested in causing mayhem and playing tricks on the living. Stacking books or chairs in piles. Banging on pipes or walls. Pulling bedclothes away in the night. All quite common descriptions of nuisance paranormal happenings, but not violent.

Had the resident spirits of 30 East Drive added hiding keys to their list of misdemeanours?

No rational explanation could be reached between the pair regarding how the keys came to be where they were found.

In fact, both were certain in their minds that the keys were left on the worktop after entering the house, as was always the case.

The ghost hunt that night turned out to be no less dramatic, but compared with a terrifying event which had unfolded in the lounge some months earlier, a set of missing keys was just child's play.

A Chair is still a Chair (even when there's no-one sitting there)

"To make a house a home, you want to feel safer there than anywhere else in the world. If you can't relax in the comfort of your own armchair then where can you be at ease?"

There are places you see – on television, in books or in person – that just scream 'I'm haunted'.

Sometimes just the look of a building can send chills running down the spine. Gothic architecture, secluded locations surrounded by woods, rickety old cottages. They all have that 'spooky' atmosphere about them, perpetuated by horror and supernatural films, and those ghost stories which gave us nightmares when we were young.

Those are the places people often assume will be haunted. But what of the regular places we encounter in our daily lives? Schools, hotels and even ordinary family homes.

Our preconceptions of a 'haunted house' are led by many external factors, but sometimes it's those perfectly innocuous places which deliver the most scares.

As children we all spent a significant part of our lives in school. A place with multiple rooms, stairwells and long corridors. At the time you probably never considered for a second that this environment had the potential to be scary. After all, when somewhere is bustling with life and noise, how could it be frightening?

But if you were to spend time in the same building without all that noise – that which makes it 'normal' – then would it *feel* different; even during the daytime?

When our surroundings are somehow out of sync with our expectations, it can totally change our perception of them.

This is very much the case at 30 East Drive.

A three bedroom semi-detached council house in the midst of a leafy suburb, surrounded by similar looking properties, inside which regular families live out their regular lives, doing regular things.

Laura Ingalls Wilder, the American writer and author of '*Little House on the Prairie*', once said, "There is no comfort anywhere for anyone who dreads to go home."

Imagine the very place that should offer you the most sanctuary, the place where you should feel at your safest, becoming your worst nightmare.

This was what the Pritchard and Hodgson families had to endure.

Even today the house retains a very strange atmosphere. Walking through the door into 30 East Drive is like stepping back in time.

A kitchen-diner, with mismatched oak units, linoleum flooring and pine wood-cladding, leads to a small lounge, in which a stone fireplace and gas-fire dominates the opposite wall.

Heavily patterned carpets – typical of the 1960s and 1970s – are fitted throughout the house. Dado rails separate floral wallpaper above from the embossed pattern below, and an old-fashioned sofa in the lounge is fringed around the base with tassels; popular in the '70s but an absolute no-no in today's interior-design conscious society.

It feels so wrong for a house which *should* carry the sounds of a happy family home to be so eerily quiet.

Perhaps it's this emptiness – in a place which should feel full of life – which makes the house feel so creepy.

Perhaps it's the stories we have all heard about the Pritchard family's experiences there.

Perhaps it really is a truly haunted house.

For one of Haunted Happenings' team members there is little doubt about the last point, after a personal experience left her completely terrified there.

After arriving at the house one night to prepare for an overnight ghost hunting event, the person in question – joined by another member of the team – was standing in the lounge.

The two were busy talking about how to plan the night and the best way to approach an investigation of the property, when something extraordinary happened.

As she turned to walk towards the door that leads back to the kitchen/diner there was a noise from behind.

She spun around to look for the source of the sound, and began to scream.

A dining-room chair had been brought through to the lounge

from the kitchen/diner for the guests to use when they arrived.

Neither of the team were within a few feet of the chair, but what they were now confronted with was something quite phenomenal.

The chair was being dragged violently across the carpeted floor, heading straight in her direction.

In complete and utter shock she ran into the next room, but the chair continued to move, as if chasing her from the lounge.

By the time it came to rest – just as abruptly as it had started moving – the chair had travelled around four feet from its original position near the armchair.

How could that happen?

Unfortunately, since the investigation wasn't even underway at this point, no audio or video recording was taking place when it happened.

To the outside world there is no evidence that this ever happened, and yet the impression it left upon them both is firmly imprinted on their minds forever.

This is often the case where poltergeist activity is concerned. It often seems that the entity cleverly chooses its moment to create mayhem, in the hope of making people blame each other for the tricks it plays.

Both the Pritchard children and their counterparts in Enfield were blamed for faking their hauntings, because the activity often happened either out of view of a camera, or the camera itself didn't record the footage.

It is these moments that we ghost hunters are always searching for, and yet we have to accept that – in the absence of hard evidence – nobody else will believe us when we share the story.

Maybe the poltergeists have mastered the art of making us look daft. Perhaps they get a kick out of seeing us blame each other for their doings.

It's possible that no matter how advanced our technology becomes, we will never gain 100% proof of their existence, because they're always one step ahead of us.

I hope that isn't the case, but only time will reveal the answer.

In the meantime the search for paranormal activity goes on, and at 30 East Drive in Pontefract, there are no shortage of screams to be had.

-11-

40 SHEEP STREET
Stratford upon Avon – Warwickshire

"During the day, I don't believe in ghosts. At night, I'm a little more open-minded." – Unknown

I t is widely believed that the world-renowned English playwright and poet, William Shakespeare, based his fictional character Sir John Falstaff on one of the residents of 40 Sheep Street; thought to be the oldest continuously lived-in house in Stratford-upon-Avon.

Some of the buildings on Sheep Street were rebuilt after a huge fire destroyed much of the town in 1595, but No. 40 – along with many others – survived the blaze, and the building we see today dates back to the year 1480.

Today the timber-framed Tudor exterior is contrasted with modern shop-frontages and popular pubs, but the history of the house – and the barn which sits at the rear of the property – is long and chequered, and full of historic importance.

It can be easy to forget just how old some of the buildings we see around us every day are, and to underestimate some of the important events and influential people who once crossed their thresholds.

Of course it's well-known that Stratford-upon-Avon is the birthplace of Sir William Shakespeare, and the town now thrives upon that fact, enjoying the many thousands of tourists it brings each year. But with so many modern buildings around, we lose touch with some of the history of the places we visit and pass each day.

Number 40 Sheep Street is still a residential address, but the huge wooden gate which sits alongside the front of the house conceals something quite wonderful.

A cobbled path leads from the gate towards the barn – now a museum centred entirely on Tudor history – and it is claimed that the bard himself walked those very cobbles, to visit the Three Tuns Tavern, which was once housed inside what is now the museum.

To be able to physically touch the very same cobbled street upon which those with such historic importance have trodden is a rare opportunity to connect with our history and its characters.

But this building has received other important visitors during its long history, including one who would go on to sign the death warrant of the king of England, Charles I.

Oliver Cromwell's name is infamous. Considered one of the most controversial figures in the history of the British Isles, he was an English military and political leader who dominated the brief period in which the country became the Commonwealth of England.

Cromwell is thought to have stayed at 40 Sheep Street in 1651. A letter written to Lord Wharton – 4th Baron of Wharton and a favourite of Cromwell's – was sent from the town of Stratford-upon-Avon on 27 August, before Cromwell left to lead the Battle of Worcester, the last of the English Civil War.

As with any building with such a lengthy history, the barn to the rear of 40 Sheep Street – now known as The Tudor World Museum – is believed to have served a number of purposes over the years; many of them dubious and often illegal.

In addition to the tavern, the building is thought to have provided a refuge for merchants to hide their goods, and also acted as a house of ill-repute, for ladies to offer their services to the gentleman-folk who visited at night.

During this period a small cottage was also attached to the end of the barn, believed to be the dwelling of the 'witch of Sheep Street'.

The local coven still reveres this area and practices their ancient ceremonies in the courtyard, outside what remains of the cottage today.

It is likely that such a property would have seen numerous horrors across the years, and some wonder whether the souls of those who lost their lives at different times in the grounds still haunt the building today.

It is claimed that a number of spirits still roam the property, and people have reported many strange sightings – both during the daytime tours and in the evenings – including that of a hooded figure, with glowing red eyes, who simply watches from a quiet corner of the building.

Often guests have reported a particularly heavy and oppressive feeling when inside the barn, especially on the upper floor, which may be attributed to the spirit of an 18th century serial-killer who is also thought to haunt the dark recesses of the building.

In addition to these two spectral beings, mediums and psychics have talked of a little girl by the name of Lucy, who was a pickpocket in the tavern, and a justice of the peace who used his power to run an extortion ring with threats, violence and trumped up charges.

Many of the characters described here are particularly

unpleasant when encountered, but one of the spirits believed to still haunt the place is the shrieve – an archer to King Henry VIII and the first recorded tenant of the building – who some believe still protects visitors to the property from those less-welcoming entities.

It is little wonder that there is so much reported activity within this building, as it sits upon no fewer than five ley lines. There are also reported to be several vortexes on the upper floors, through which non-grounded spirits can enter and leave again, making it a real hot-spot for paranormal activity.

Inside the barn visitors are greeted by an eerie scene. Low beams and uneven floors make for a claustrophobic atmosphere, even for the most average-height adult, and the darkened passageways which lead from one area to another are separated by black-out drapes, through which one has to pass to access the rooms.

Displays depicting the horrors of the Black Death greet the eyes as you climb the wooden staircase which leads to the upper floor. In one recess stands the figure of a plague doctor, complete with the instantly recognisable wax jacket and beaked mask; a truly menacing and spooky visual reminder of one of our country's darkest moments.

However, one of the most intriguing and active areas of the whole property lies tucked away in the attic, accessed only by ladder-style wooden steps.

And this room has a few stories to tell.

The Séance Room

On Halloween night in 2017, a small group of ghost hunters made their way up the steps and gathered around the huge séance table which sits in the room.

Nestled into the eaves of the barn, the Séance room – as it is now referred – is a small and incredibly dark space, used partly for storage of the many display items belonging to the museum downstairs.

The table can seat up to sixteen participants, and the group had decided to conduct a traditional Victorian séance in an attempt to illicit some paranormal activity.

With everybody settled into their seats and a number of EMF meters and trigger objects in place, they began calling out to the spirits of the building to make themselves known.

As on most occasions, it took time before anybody in the room began to report anything strange, but it did come.

'I can feel pressure on my hand,' one of the group announced.

'I just felt a thump on the table,' came another.

One by one people began to sense and feel that something within the space had changed. A heavy atmosphere shrouded the room which hadn't been felt at the beginning, and it was about to get more intense.

The museum exhibits are stacked along each side of the room, in the space between the entrance to the attic and where the table is positioned.

A collection of weird and wonderful Tudor-style artefacts lay in large heaps, with dismembered mannequins staring from the piles; arms and legs reaching out at angles, as if pleading for help.

To access the table you have to pass the items and climb across a supporting metal beam, so by the time the séance was underway, nobody was any closer to the curiosities than around four feet.

With none of the gadgets or trigger objects registering any changes in the immediate area around the table, the blackness of the room had completely immersed the group. Nothing was visible to the naked eye, the only respite being the dim glow of an emergency exit sign, positioned upon one of the beams.

Then, out of the darkness it came.

Somewhere near the doorway which leads back to the steps, a huge crash was heard.

From within the pile of museum items the noise penetrated the silence of the room, sending a wave of fear and shock through the whole group.

It was clear that the sound had come from somewhere amongst the stack on the right hand side of the room, but we couldn't be certain what had been moved.

However, just prior to the noise two members of the group involved in the séance had begun to notice what they described as movement in that same direction. Barely perceptible in the darkness, they were just in the process of trying to describe to the group where they were looking, and that's exactly the moment when it happened.

Bang.

Of course, as with all investigations of potential paranormal activity, the first reaction by the host was to hush the group and request for it to happen again.

'If that was somebody trying to get our attention then please do it again!'

Silence.

The requests didn't produced any further noises from the corner, so the next step was to explore the pile where the noise had come from, to see if it was obvious what had been moved.

Again, no firm answer could be found. But, the question of how it had happened also remained unanswered.

With fourteen people walking past the pile it seemed perfectly logical that something could easily dislodge and fall. The wooden flooring of the séance room could easily have created enough movement to make something move while the group moved into position.

However, having been sitting perfectly still for more than fifteen minutes prior to the sound, this now seemed far less likely.

Add to this the 'coincidence' that two members of the group had just noticed a shadowy movement in the same area of the room, and they were left with the assumption that, perhaps, they had just encountered something paranormal.

One of the benefits of investigating a location on a number of separate occasions, as the team who lead these events often have, is that you begin to notice similarities with past experiences.

And, unbeknown to the majority of the group, the host was aware that around two years prior to this night, something very similar had occurred in the very same room.

The events leading up to the first encounter were very similar. A dozen guests, joined by two team members leading the ghost hunt, were seated around the same table.

On this occasion the temperature in the room was significantly warmer thanks to the balmy mid-summer temperatures outside, but due to the lateness of the hour, the darkness was no less intense.

Around the room – behind the seating and fixed to the wall – sits a shelf, upon which a number of picture frames stand.

The pitch of the ceiling leans into the room at around forty-five degrees at the point where the shelves are positioned, and most of the photographs sit upon the shelf, leaning back against the ceiling structure.

After a period of inactivity, and just prior to the group giving up and returning to the base room for coffee, all hell broke loose.

Sitting in the darkness of a reportedly haunted building – in which many menacing encounters have been reported – and hearing the crash of something being thrown is utterly terrifying; especially mid-way through a séance.

Fear will most likely surge through the body. Some will respond with a scream which, in turn, will intensify the fear amongst others, who may assume something else is happening to those around them other than what they themselves had heard. The desire to flee may overwhelm you, but then you realise that there is nowhere to run.

It is pitch black.

Once the group had managed to turn on their torches and investigate the surroundings, it became obvious that one of the photographs was now face down on the shelf.

'Was this picture like this when we came in?' someone asked.

'Nope. It was definitely standing up.' another one replied. 'I know for sure because we looked at them before we sat down to see who they were of.'

'That's right,' came another voice. 'We did the same.'

Closer inspection revealed that the picture didn't have a stand and had therefore been propped against the eaves at an angle.

If the photograph had simply slipped down from its position, it would have been facing upwards. But it wasn't. It was face down on the shelf, meaning that it had been tipped up deliberately.

But by whom?

Suspicion naturally falls upon those closest to the item. The brain's desire to find a logical reason – or basically somebody to blame – is overwhelming.

However, at the time this happened everyone within reaching distance of the picture were seated with their backs towards the shelf.

As part of the séance everybody's hands were positioned on the table, and with some ambient light coming from the glow of the EMF meters it would be impossible for anyone to turn around and push the photograph without being detected. Even in complete darkness, the chair would have creaked and the people either side of the culprit would have spotted their movement.

Everyone attested to the fact that nobody had moved a muscle, and that their little fingers had remained in contact on the table throughout the whole vigil.

Whoever or whatever it was that caused the picture to end up face-down on the shelf that night we will never be sure.

But what we do know is that, on at least two occasions in the séance room, items appear to have moved of their own accord – even when the group have been seated deathly still for ages beforehand.

Does the attic room of 40 Sheep Street have a resident poltergeist? I wouldn't like to go up there alone and find out!

Party on the 1ˢᵗ Floor

Every building is different and presents its own unique set of problems to a paranormal investigator.

Stately homes, once secluded in their own grounds, now find themselves surrounded by busy housing estates. Pubs and inns which used to welcome horse-drawn carriages are often now subjected to noise pollution from the modern car and busier roads. Places which would once have been black in the dead of night may now suffer from light pollution from nearby street lights.

Of course this doesn't mean that they can't be haunted. However, it may make it a little more difficult for those seeking evidence of paranormal activity to distinguish between external sounds from the living, versus those from within the building, hopefully created by the dead.

40 Sheep Street is no different.

Sited in a bustling area of the town, and positioned nearby to two busy pubs, the beginning of an investigation may encounter some noise pollution. The trick is to work around these issues and explore experiments at the time which aren't affected by the external influences, then wait until everything outside has gone quiet before concentrating on the auditory phenomena.

One such method of contact which is often called upon during these moments is table tipping; a traditional experiment where the participants will place their hands lightly upon the surface of a small table and request that the spirits attempt to make a knock on the surface or, even better, actually move or tilt the table beneath people's hands.

Early one evening in 2014 – during a table tipping vigil – something very odd happened.

On the upper floor there is a landing area, accessed by the main wooden staircase, and beneath this area is the entrance to the museum – the gift shop.

In order to minimise any noise pollution the three small groups who were working in the building separated into different areas. One had moved to the far end of the building, while another had gone to the upper floor landing. The final group had opted to try a table tipping experiment in the shop area on the ground floor.

Understanding that any movement from those on the landing would be heard by those below, it was decided to carry out a glass divination experiment upstairs, to minimise the need for people to move around.

Neither of the vigils produced a great deal of activity. The glass moved slightly on the table upstairs, edging towards one corner and then back again, but no real 'communication' was achieved, and we were not able to ask any questions of whoever it was that may have been with us.

Downstairs in the shop area the situation was similar. One or two knocks had been heard, seemingly from beneath the surface, and people had reported feeling that the table seemed to be trembling at times, but nothing else of any significance happened.

As the guests headed back to the base room for a coffee break – feeling slightly disappointed at the initial lack of activity – the three team members gathered to compare notes about the first vigil.

And it was during that conversation that they realised something strange had been going on right under their eyes.

'How did your sessions go?' the host asked.

'Not as good as yours by the sound of it,' one of the others replied.

The host looked puzzled.

'What do you mean?' he asked.

'We were down in the shop, underneath you,' the other team member began. 'We could hear you all moving around upstairs. It sounded like you were chasing the bloody table around the room, but all we got were a few taps and knocks.'

The host stared blankly, looking completely baffled.

'We weren't moving around,' he replied. 'In fact, hardly anything happened for us either, but we remained *really* still while doing some glass divination so that we didn't make too much noise for you.'

Things were getting weird.

'So you weren't doing table tipping up there?'

'Nope,' he replied. 'We were stood really still all the way through. People will have moved from foot to foot to keep comfortable while standing around the table, but nobody was walking around at all, I swear.'

The team member who'd been working in the shop pulled one of the guests from her group into the conversation.

'Tell him what we heard from upstairs during that first vigil,' she urged.

The guest, a young man and self-confessed sceptic at the beginning of the night, explained.

'We could hear you lot thundering around up there,' he began. 'Was there a party on the 1st floor we weren't invited to?'

After involving people from each of the groups into the conversation, it became clear that everyone downstairs in the shop had heard those above "thundering around". They insisted it had lasted for at least five minutes, towards the end of the vigil.

Those from the group upstairs all agreed there was no way that they had created anywhere near the noise the other group was describing.

So what had they heard?

To clarify the situation we took everybody back to the same places and recreated the movement.

This time, those downstairs confirmed they heard nothing more than the faintest footstep or creak of the wooden floor.

What happened that night was totally baffling.

Had only one person reported hearing something you would probably question their judgement. But seven people reported heavy footsteps from above them, where nobody was moving around.

How do you explain that?

They couldn't, and to this day it remains yet another mystery. Just one more curious encounter in the dark recesses of 40 Sheep Street.

When Time Stood Still

In any walk of life, to have your notions challenged and be faced with a situation which makes you question the very foundations of your belief system is a red-letter moment.

Whether you've actively gone in search of those questions, or had them thrust upon you unexpectedly, is neither here nor there. Our beliefs and opinions are personal to us, so when rocked by a revelation to the contrary it can be very disconcerting, and force us to ask ourselves some serious questions.

When those beliefs are related to the subject of the paranormal, and the experience is a personal one – sometimes frightening – then it can leave us very confused.

Many years prior to those sounds of footsteps and the apparent poltergeist activity in the attic, a ghost hunting guest was faced one such experience, which went on to leave a lasting impression – and ignited a passion for exploring paranormal activity in many locations across the country.

The evening had begun as usual. A number of guests arrived, some looking rather nervous and others bubbling with excitement at the prospect of what lay ahead in the darkness of the barn.

During the introductions the host had asked the group about their individual beliefs regarding spirits and ghosts. There was nothing abnormal in this question, but merely to give an indication of what people's approaches to the night may be.

As is often the case a number of people held up their hand to indicate they'd previously experienced things which they believed were paranormal, while a few proudly confessed that – although they were here to take part in a ghost hunt – they were very sceptical about the whole affair, and would require something truly inexplicable to happen in order for them to alter those beliefs.

It didn't take long for one such moment to occur, but the manner in which it happened was something that none of the team that night were quite prepared for, and hadn't experienced before.

Over the years one particular area of the barn at 40 Sheep Street has stood out as unusual for the hosts who have been there several times.

At the end of the main landing – accessed by the main staircase – a blackout curtain hangs across an open doorframe, leading to an area where it's possible for a small group to gather.

As with the whole museum, this space is decked-out with authentic visual representations of Tudor times.

Wooden beams with flaking whitewash paint, waxworks of

infamous characters such as Queen Elizabeth I and her mystical advisor John Dee, various trinkets and mock-ups of shop frontages, complete with lead-work window frames. It's all there.

The surroundings offer a real insight into the lives of the Tudors, and when the lights are switched off the whole building takes on a very foreboding atmosphere.

Truly spooky!

This particular space has been the one area of the property where, over the years, several completely unconnected people have reported experiencing physical contact and sensations.

From an overwhelming feeling of dread and fear, to the sensation of being touched and grabbed by unseen hands. People's moods have changed without warning and many have been overcome with emotion, for which they can offer no explanation.

But crucially – because these experiences have happened many months apart and with people who have never met each other – there could be no expectations in the minds of the participants when they first enter this space.

This is important because, as has been proven many times, our preconceptions will affect our behaviour and the resulting outcome of the moment.

On this particular night I'd led a small number of guests into this area to carry out a short watch and wait vigil; no gadgets or clever equipment, just real people wishing to make contact with the 'other side'.

We formed a circle and linked our hands, in the hope of providing the spirits with plenty of energy to use as a method of contact (but also to rule out the possibility of any pranks). If anybody reported the feeling of being touched then we wanted them to be able to be certain in their own minds that it wasn't one of the group being a bit naughty.

Less than two or three minutes had passed before all hell broke loose.

Just behind the circle on one side of the room was some fake ivy foliage, climbing the framework of one of the exhibits.

In the all-consuming blackness of the room, while listening intently for any sounds that could potentially be paranormal in its origin, the sound of rustling was heard.

'Did anybody hear that?' I asked. 'Is somebody leaning against something?'

But there was no answer.

It was that exact moment, just as the words had left my mouth, when I felt something which sent absolute fear into my very soul.

I felt the full force of a body slamming into me.

Having never had that personal interaction we all seek before, where you actually feel the sensation of being grabbed or touched by an unseen force, this was a first for me.

I'm not easily frightened and will quite happily wander alone through any of those 'haunted' buildings in which the team regularly spend their weekends, but in the total darkness of The Tudor World Museum – full of anticipation and knowledge of the things that had gone before in this space – I felt true fear.

It's incredible how quickly the mind can process thoughts.

What the hell was that?

Did anybody else feel what I just felt?

I need to get my torch!

All of these things ran through my mind within a split-second, and at exactly the same moment, the panic began.

Everyone had heard the sound and knew something was happening, but in the darkness nobody knew just what was going on.

It could only have taken a maximum of two seconds before my hand had broken loose of the people either side of me, desperately reaching into my pocket to find the torch and get some light on the situation.

There, laying on the floor right at my feet, was one of the guests.

She's unconscious!

The absolute horror of realising that one of the guests – whose safety I was responsible for – had passed out and potentially hurt themselves was mixed with the instant relief that there was a perfectly natural explanation for what I'd just felt myself.

Instinct kicked in and I set about dealing with the situation at hand. The priority now was to look after the lady who, I presumed at the time, had fainted and fallen forwards – bumping into me on the way down.

Thankfully, after just a couple of seconds this poor lady regained consciousness and was soon able to sit upright again, showing no signs of any serious injury.

'Do you feel able to stand so that we can help you downstairs?' I asked.

The look on her face is something that has remained with me ever since. Eyes wide, staring straight through me as if looking at the space beyond. She didn't respond.

Instead, she went limp once again.

'Right, we need to get her out of here now!' I said, realising that this was now potentially quite urgent.

It was quite possible (even probable) that she had simply fainted. After all, the space was quite small and with a number of bodies gathered together, combined with the layers of clothing we were all wearing, it was likely that she had overheated.

But there was one other alternative swirling throughout my head. One that I really didn't want to consider, but *had* to deal with right now – just in case!

Having led literally dozens of ghost hunts at this building before that night, and knowing the history of what others had reported while in this space, I had to consider the possibility that she'd had some sort of reaction to the energy of the room – possibly that of a negative spirit.

If this was the case then I needed her out of the area, and quick. I needed to remove her from the energy which may be affecting her, so that I could ensure she came to no further harm, and make a proper assessment of the situation.

As we began to lift her she once again regained consciousness, but as we helped the lady to her feet – to assist her in getting her out of the building and into the fresh air – she slumped into our arms.

'Just grab her please,' I urged two of the men in the group. 'I need help getting her down the steps safely and outside.'

It took three men to get her carefully down the stairs, through the shop area, and out into the courtyard, where she was able to sit on the wooden platform and get some air.

After a few minutes, and plenty of cold water, she seemed absolutely fine and was able to answer a few questions.

'Has this ever happened before?' I asked.

'No,' I've never done a ghost hunt before, but have never fainted either – to my knowledge.'

'Did you eat before coming here tonight?'

'Yeah,' she replied. 'We had a meal in the pub before coming.'

'Any history in the family you're aware of, or any medical conditions I should know about?' I continued – aware I was now firing question after question at the poor soul in a desperate attempt to find a perfectly logical answer to the situation.

'No – I'm fit and healthy.'

'So, what happened?' I asked.

And that's when it got even weirder.

She went on to explain that she remembered standing in the room for a while, with nothing happening. She added it wasn't until we all started to leave the room she just came over very 'strange', and then the next thing she was aware of was being on the floor.

I stopped her mid-flow, puzzled.

'What do you mean, when we all started to leave?' I asked, assuming she was just confused about the events leading up to the incident. 'We'd only just started the séance.'

The look of confusion was now hers.

She remained absolutely adamant that we had been in the room for at least ten minutes, trying to make contact, and that we'd decided to give up and head into another area. But this was absolutely not the case.

It only took a few minutes of being outside before she confirmed she felt absolutely fine and – some would say bravely – that she not only wanted to continue with the ghost hunt, but also wanted to go back to the same room.

Reluctantly I agreed that, providing the couple she was there with would keep a close eye on her for the rest of the night, she could continue as planned. The lady went on to take part in other experiments, in different parts of the building, with no further issues.

Until it was time to return to *that* room.

Once again, within moments of entering the space in which she'd had her unexplained experience, her legs went to jelly and her friends had to support her weight and lead her from the area.

No sooner was she out of the space than she felt fine.

I was confused, but absolutely convinced now that there was something strange going on. Something (or someone) in that particular part of the barn at 40 Sheep Street was affecting this person, and even though she felt fine in the rest of the building, she just wasn't safe there.

We agreed that she would avoid this room for the remainder of the night, and thankfully no further problems were encountered.

As hosts for paranormal ghost hunting events, it is impossible to know the backgrounds of those in attendance. There is no way of knowing whether anyone taking part has any tendencies for drama, any undeclared medical conditions, or even any psychological issues which may affect their experience.

We have to take people on face value, and 99% of those who join the group are absolutely fine.

In this case the lady in question was not prone to drama or exaggeration. She is a perfectly level-headed and intelligent individual who just wanted to take part in this unusual experience and see for herself what it was like.

In fact, one of the hands which was raised at the start of the night in declaration of being sceptical was hers. She maintained that she'd come with an open mind but didn't really believe that ghosts or spirits existed, and certainly didn't expect to have any sort of personal encounter which would change her mind.

How wrong she was.

This lady has since gone on to join Haunted Happenings on a number of other ghost hunts across the years and, despite visiting lots of reputedly haunted locations, has never had another episode like the one that night at 40 Sheep Street.

Whether or not the guests on these events experience something that changes their viewpoint is really of no concern to the company. Providing everyone enjoys the process of taking part and makes their own mind up about anything that does happen, the owner of Haunted Happenings – and the teams who host the events – is happy.

Sadly we will never know for sure what happened in that room and why this one guest was so badly affected, but having ruled out all other possibilities, both she and I concluded that it was likely to have been something paranormal.

Either way, it was a night neither of us will ever forget!

PENDLE HILL
Clitheroe – Lancashire

A place of mystery and pride
Sweet Pendle has a past to hide
For witches once resided here
And locals' hearts ran cold with fear

One night in March it all began
The night ill-fate befell a man
A witches curse, he would proclaim
In 1612 they were to blame

From Malkin Tower, a lowly place
Began the witches' fall from grace
Ten would hang 'til dead, at dawn
The Pendle Witches' legend borne

But Pendle isn't just a place
Where those accused would fall from grace
The hill, they say, is one to fear
For ghosts of witches may appear

A dense mist hung heavy across the landscape, shrouding the moorland around us in a blanket of fog. But for the sounds of distant sheep and occasional wildlife, the silence on the hill was deafening.

The moon, which should have provided us with some welcome light upon the otherwise dark scrubland, served only to illuminate the fog, creating an eerie glow in which spectral figures seemed to dance and twirl to silent music.

This isolated spot, far from the flickering lights of the towns below, was my first experience of the infamous Pendle Hill – a place with a terrible history; now allegedly haunted by the ghosts of witches.

The Pendle Witch Trials of 1612

The Pendle Witch trials have long fascinated those with a thirst for history, and people who live in and around the area are very much aware of the fate of the unfortunate souls accused of witchcraft back in 1612.

But for the majority the witches' story first came to the forefront of our minds in April 2005, when the *Most Haunted* crew descended upon the hill in the search for evidence of paranormal activity.

Ever since those episodes aired, the story of the Pendle Witch Trials has ignited interest in the paranormal world, with hundreds upon hundreds of ghost hunters making their way out onto the hill at night – in search of ghosts – over the last thirteen years.

The story began when a peddler by the name of John Law claimed to have been injured by witchcraft, after refusing to provide a local girl, Alison Device, with some pins.

He asserted that, in retaliation for his refusal, the girl had cast a spell upon him which had left him lame.

In reality Law had probably suffered a stroke, but Alison herself was convinced that she had supernatural powers, having sold her soul to the devil, and it was her own confession which brought about the charges.

Alison's grandmother, Elizabeth Southerns (known as Old Demdike), had long been considered a witch by locals, and the events which unfolded implicated not only Demdike, but the rest of the family too.

A long-held feud between the Southerns and the local Whittle family, of which Anne Whittle (Old Chattox) was matriarch – resulted in accusations being levelled towards them also.

On 2 April 1612 Demdike, Chattox and Chattox's daughter were summoned before a justice of the peace, where damning confessions were made by the two old ladies.

They confessed that they'd sold their souls in return for higher powers, and Demdike also implicated Anne Redferne, with a statement saying she'd witnessed her making clay figures – to be used to inflict injury towards others via witchcraft.

The story may have ended with the trials of those three women, but a meeting at Malkin Tower – the home of Old Demdike – on Good Friday in 1612, led to further investigation of the families and further accusations.

It was that meeting which escalated the situation, and ultimately resulted in the execution of ten of the accused, who hanged by the neck until dead.

Malkin Tower is believed to have been demolished soon after the trials in 1612, and there are differing opinions about the location on which it once stood.

Simon Entwistle, a local historian and Pendle Witch expert, has his own theories, and for many years has been accompanying Haunted Happenings' tours to the area on Pendle Hill.

Through his company Top Hat Tours, Simon delivers guided excursions of the Ribble Valley and surrounding areas, providing unique and exciting insights into the area's rich and mystical histories. He has made numerous television and radio appearances doing what he does best; story telling with passion.

To venture onto Pendle Hill in the dead of night is itself unique and exciting, but what could one really expect to encounter in terms of paranormal activity when out on the moors after dark?

You may be surprised!

In the early days of public ghost hunts the equipment available was fairly limited.

Mostly investigations would focus upon the traditional Victorian techniques of séances – including table tipping, glass divination and Ouija board experiments – but these would naturally be difficult to carry out in a rural environment such as Pendle Hill, with uneven ground and potentially inclement weather to content with.

In recent years more and more affordable gadgets have come onto the market, such as K2 meters and EDI meters, which have allowed any ghost hunter the chance to add a more scientific element to their investigations.

Of course, a flashing light to indicate an increase in EMF energy isn't proof of a spectral presence on its own, but when combined with a number of other factors it can certainly add weight to the possibility.

When using such equipment it is critical to ensure that base-line tests are carried out. For example, you'd want to be sure that the spike in energy you're hoping is something of paranormal origin, isn't actually coming from an electrical current somewhere in a building, or from a mobile phone receiving a message or call.

For that reason, before utilising such technology in an investigation, the area would be checked for any obvious causes of interference, and all mobile devices would be switched off.

Inside a building, where cables could be out of sight and electricity is all around us, this may still not guarantee that the energy change isn't man-made. So when you're out on a hill, miles from civilisation and with no power nearby, you wouldn't expect these pieces of equipment to register any activity at all.

But they have! On many occasions.

During many watch and wait vigils on Pendle Hill, groups have witnessed significant changes in the EMF energy when calling out for spirits to make their presence known.

On one cold February night, the group had formed a circle and placed an EMF meter onto the ground in the centre.

In order to validate any spikes which may later happen, the group left the device there for several minutes before starting the vigil, just to make sure the base-line reading was flat.

During this time Simon, the historian, regaled the group with the fascinating story of the witches, setting the scene for the ghost hunting which would follow shortly.

There were no EMF spikes during this time.

But then the vigil began.

'If there's anybody here with us on the hill now, please come forward and make yourself known,' one of the team began. 'We are not here to judge or offend you, we'd just like to know you're there.'

The anticipation of this moment is palpable. For those who have attended ghost hunts before there is an excitement of what may come, and for those taking part for the first time, there's often an element of fear. Either way, you can almost cut the tension with a knife while waiting in silence for any response.

It was just a matter of moments before something quite extraordinary happened.

The lights on the K2 meter began to flicker; gently at first, and then increasing in their intensity until all the way up to the red.

'Oh my God,' someone blurted out. 'Is this for real?'

The K2 meter has become hugely popular with ghost hunters

and paranormal investigators, as it provides a simple, visual way of confirming a change of energy in the immediate vicinity of the device.

In this situation, the highest reading would indicate the electromagnetic field near the meter had suddenly increased to over 20 MilliGAUSS.

To put this into perspective, you would normally need to hold the device within inches of a power cable to illicit the same level of response.

But they were out on Pendle Hill and all mobile phones were switched off.

Perhaps it's just faulty?

This is a perfectly natural response and exactly what one should consider. After all, there's no point in assuming *everything* is paranormal, otherwise the very word becomes redundant – how can something which is 'normal' be 'para-normal'?

In order to test this the group tried to gain intelligent responses from the timings of the flashes.

'If that's you making those lights blink, then could you please step away for a moment so they stop?'

The lights went out, returning to the single green light which indicates the device is on.

'Wow!' someone said. Then, after a moment or two without any responses, they continued.

'I'm sorry to ask, but could I ask you to step closer again so we can see the lights go back up?'

The light returned to red and the group gasped.

But that wasn't the end, because while they continued with this interaction, a lady in the group spoke up.

'Can anybody else smell that?' she asked.

'I can smell flowers, or a strong floral perfume,' another guest replied instantly.

Suddenly, as if from nowhere, the whole area surrounding the group had become infused with a very sweet, floral fragrance. It was as if somebody had brushed against a scented flowerbed and a light breeze had wafted it into their midst.

Now of course flowers grow in the wild, so it could be possible that this was something natural. But it's worth remembering that this was around 12.30am, with a reasonable breeze blowing, and it was still early-February.

Had it been a summer's daytime, the scent of flowers drifting amongst them wouldn't have even raised an eyebrow, but at night it was a different story.

Also, with the breeze as it was, you wouldn't expect a waft of flowers to hang in the air, which is exactly what happened. It lingered for around twenty seconds, then vanished without fanfare. As suddenly as it had arrived, it was now gone again.

People sniffed each other to confirm that nobody in the group was wearing a strong perfume which could have been the cause.

There were not.

Each of these elements in their solitude would not necessarily be of any real significance. But with the sudden changes in electromagnetic readings, combined with the appearance of a sweet scent – right at the moment when the group began asking for a sign of somebody's presence – it becomes more interesting.

Were the three just coincidence? Was there a perfectly plausible explanation for those moments? None could be found at the time, and so it is left up to those in attendance on the night to make their own minds up.

Either way, spending time upon Pendle Hill at night – whatever the season – is a magical, eerie and sometimes frightening experience. Perhaps you'll encounter the ghosts of Old Demdike and Old Chattox.

Maybe you'll spot the mysterious black dog which Alison Device believed to be her 'familiar' and the cause of John Law's mysterious ailment, or hear the creaking of the rope from which ten witches were hanged in 1612.

Dread at the Dunkenhalgh

In 2013, with the popularity of ghost hunts upon Pendle Hill showing no signs of waning, the company decided to expand the Pendle experience to include a weekend break at the Dunkenhalgh hotel in nearby Clayton-le Moors, Blackburn.

The hotel itself was once a country manor house, dating back to the end of the 12th century.

Originally built by Roger de Dunkenhalgh, the property has changed hands several times, and the current building dates predominantly from the 19th century, while incorporating parts of 16th century construction.

The elegant sandstone façade is flanked by two outer-bay towers, the eastern side having crow-stepped parapets, giving a castle-like appearance to the property.

Inside, a grand 18th century staircase leads from the entrance hall to the first floor, and downstairs the Portrait Room houses paintings of former owners and their families; the perfect setting for Hercule Poirot or Miss Marple to reveal the identity of a killer.

Today it's a luxurious spa-hotel, but as with any old building there is no shortage of ghostly sightings and strange happenings.

Local legend has it that those forced to pass near the hotel after nightfall would make furtive glances in its direction, eager to make haste and put the property firmly behind them; especially on Christmas Eve.

It is said that the ghost of a woman wearing a white gown is seen moving along the tree-line near the site of a bridge in the grounds, before disappearing from sight without a trace.

The girl is thought to be that of a French governess by the

name of Lucette, who allegedly threw herself into the raging torrent one stormy night after her heart was broken by a young officer.

The story goes that he deceived her, and believing there was no future for her now at the estate, she decided to end her own life.

Her ghost is said to haunt the scene of her demise on Christmas Eve, and there have been numerous alleged sightings of the poor soul which have left those who have seen her feeling absolutely terrified.

You only have to look online to find comment after comment from people who claim to have had ghostly experiences at the Dunkenhalgh Hotel.

From table silverware being mixed up when staff have left the room, to sightings of a woman on the end of the bed in room 2, there is no shortage of stories from staff and visitors alike.

But it was in the early hours of Sunday 19 May 2013 – as the first Pendle Witch Weekend ghost hunting tour came to a close – that something very odd happened.

Most of the guests had retired to their rooms at 3am, and all that was left for me to do was clear away the equipment from the Portrait Room, which had acted as our base for the night.

One group of four guests – two ladies and two gents – had missed out on something intriguing which had happened earlier that night in Room 16 upstairs.

These two couples were regulars with Haunted Happenings and were known to me, so while I continued to tidy up downstairs they were given the key to this room so that they could go and investigate alone for twenty minutes.

None of them had ever been known to exaggerate their experiences on any previous events, and one of the men in particular considered himself quite sceptical when it came to all things paranormal. In short, they were all very level headed people and experienced ghost hunters.

I was incredibly surprised when I ascended the staircase to let them know I'd finished and would require the room card back, to find them standing in the corridor outside the room.

'Everything okay?' I asked them, curious as to why they were outside when they'd been so keen to spend time in there.

'Not really,' one of the ladies began. 'We went in there but all felt really uncomfortable straight away. We tried to do a vigil but were all too frightened.'

Knowing these people as I do, this came as a big surprise. They had all taken an active part in vigils throughout the weekend and none had ever mentioned feeling or sensing anything at any point, so for four adults to tell me they were scared in that room was a little strange.

In fact, the sceptical man was standing with one foot in the room and the other in the hallway when I arrived.

'Why are you standing like that?' I asked.

'To be honest with you mate, I really want to go in, but whenever I do I just burst into tears. It's really bizarre. I never cry and for some reason I just feel completely distraught when I'm in there.'

I was completely baffled, but with some coaxing they agreed to face their fears and we entered the room together.

The whole time we were in there, their gaze was being drawn to the bathroom door in the far corner, as if they were all expecting someone to appear in the doorway at any moment.

'Would you like to try using the Ouija board before we wrap up?' I offered, slightly curious to see whether anything interesting would happen since they all seemed so badly affected by the room.

'Sure, let's do it,' they agreed.

What happened next was even stranger than what had gone before.

The glass on the board moved quite freely beneath their fingers, and after a few moments it began moving towards me.

'Are you related to Wayne?' one of them asked.

'N-O' came the reply. The word S-A-F-E was then spelled on the board.

'Do you feel safe with Wayne here?' they asked.

'Y-E-S'.

Have you tried to make yourself known to any of us already?'

'L-I-G-H-T'

That was when I shuddered!

It is important not to make anything 'fit' when making use of the Ouija board, but there was something I hadn't told anyone throughout the weekend which now seemed relevant.

That weekend I was sleeping in Room 14, just down the corridor. The room is stunning and very spacious, with a three-seater sofa tucked away in one corner, and a beautifully ornate fireplace on the opposite wall to the bed.

On three separate occasions over the course of my stay I had returned to my room to find the light on.

I was absolutely sure I'd turned it off, but made the assumption on the first occasion that perhaps the housekeeping team had been in and had accidentally left it switched on.

The second time it happened I had only popped out of the room for a matter of minutes, to speak to the reception desk about the evening meal ahead, so I was certain that nobody had been in the room in that short space of time.

When it happened for a third time my suspicions were truly aroused that perhaps something paranormal was happening.

But I hadn't told anyone. Not a soul. Not even one of the other team members.

They can't be tricking me because nobody knows about it.

'Have you tried to make yourself known to me this weekend?' I asked tentatively, truly hoping that the answer would be no, as I had to go back to this room on my own shortly, to get some sleep before the long drive home in what was now just a few hours.

'Y-E-S'

'Did you turn on the light in my room?' I asked.

'Y-E-S'.

The four of them looked at me, completely amazed, as I explained what had happened over the weekend.

When moments like this happen I'm left scratching my head. To be singled out by the movement of the glass is one thing, but to then have a very specific word spelled out which I could relate to, but that nobody else would know anything about, was truly strange.

As we wrapped up the conversation with this entity, they asked one further question.

'Are you going to make yourself known to Wayne when he goes back to the room now?'

The feeling which went through me as the letters were spelled out on the board is one I won't forget in a hurry.

'Y-E-S'

Feeling completely bemused, and ridiculously tired, we retired to our rooms, and for as much as I'd like to say I saw a ghost that night, I didn't.

My head hit the pillow and I was out for the count.

Perhaps he tried. Perhaps he didn't. Perhaps it was all just in my head, or a wonderful coincidence.

Either way, I slept well and woke to find the bedroom light still off.

My stay at the Dunkenhalgh Hotel in Blackburn had certainly been eventful and had left me with more questions than answers.

I would love to return one day, although perhaps I'll ask for a different room next time....just in case!

-13-

DRACULA'S CASTLE
Bran – Transylvania

Since my ghost hunting journey began in 2009 I have been extremely fortunate to see some amazing places and experience things few people ever will.

I've been locked in medieval dungeons, spent time in empty prison cells, wandered the corridors of historic castles, and encountered a different kind of spirits in many reportedly haunted pubs and inns around the UK.

But in April 2015 I was given the opportunity to take ghost hunting to a completely new level. To venture into the depths of Romania; into the heartland of myths and legends of vampires and werewolves.

The location, the world-renowned Bran Castle – thought by some to be the inspiration for the home of the title character in Bram Stoker's *Dracula*.

I'm somewhat ashamed to say I'd never read the novel (I have since), although I was fully aware of the legend of this infamous Vampire Count's wicked, bloodthirsty ways.

Whether based on fiction or not, this would be an experience like no other; a location few will ever have the opportunity to investigate in such an intimate group.

Bran Castle is a Romanian national monument, situated near Brașov, on the border of the Transylvania and Wallachia regions of the country.

The first documented mention of Bran Castle dates back to 1377, although the Teutonic Knights had previously built a wooden fortress on the same site in the early 13th century. The stone fortress we see today was used in defence against the Ottoman Empire, and played a strategic military role right up until the mid-18th century.

Today, the castle is a museum dedicated to the display of furniture and art collected by the last Queen of Romania; Queen Marie.

Bran Castle is a sight to behold; a remarkable Gothic design constructed of wood and stone, built into a jagged cliff's edge, towering 60ft above the town below.

A distinctive turreted red roof sits atop the castle's thick walls, into which are spliced narrow openings for archers and cannons, with iron grates over the portals and hidden passageways built into them.

Inside, a complex series of passages and staircases link the many rooms, with whitewashed walls and stunning period furniture throughout.

Overlooking the courtyard, off which the castle's chapel can be found, is a room in which medieval torture equipment is housed; some replica and some original.

The depravity and horrors of times gone by are displayed for all to see, and it was in this room that one of the most frightening encounters I've ever experienced was about to happen.

The Torture Room

As we neared the end of what was already an eye-opening experience at Bran Castle, the group I was working with were standing in a circle – hands connected – surrounded by these barbaric instruments of torture and death.

A short while into the vigil many of the group became aware of a noise from the corner of the room, seemingly emanating from one of the pieces of equipment.

The Rack, considered one of the most feared methods of torture in England, was employed as a method of extracting information during medieval times.

The poor victim would be strapped upon a huge piece of wood, arms and legs tied with rope to the four corners, which were attached to two giant rollers. A handle at each end would turn the wheel, thus tightening the ropes and stretching the limbs, causing excruciating pain.

Ligaments would tear, muscles would rip apart and limbs would literally be pulled from their joints, dislocating arms, legs and shoulders with each slow, agonising turn.

It was a method reserved for those believed to be withholding information pertinent to issues of treason; crimes or plots against King and country.

They were utterly barbaric pieces of equipment and here, in the very room in which we were carrying out this night-time vigil, we were standing right beside one, convinced we could hear a noise which sounded like the creaking of a tightening rope, emanating from its position.

'Shhhhhh,' came one of the voices from within our group. 'I can hear something.'

We all listened, our hushed voices creating a deafening silence. *Creak…creak…creak*

'Did you hear it?' came another.

'Yeah, it's coming from over here, right behind me,' came one of the men's voices, standing with his back to the equipment in question.

It went silent!

We waited with bated breath for a few seconds, before calling out to the spirits.

'If there's somebody here with us who's connected to this place, please could you make that noise again?'

I'll admit now, the sceptic within me didn't expect it to happen, assuming it had just been a random noise misinterpreted by our eager senses.

Then it came again.

'Oh my God. It's definitely coming from over here,' came the man's voice again. 'It's right behind me.'

We listened intently for a couple of minutes, asking for the noise to be repeated, and each time we asked it was heard again by the majority of the group.

Those standing farthest away couldn't hear the sound, so it was suggested that we all change positions within the room and re-form the circle.

We released hands and started to move.

As a company Haunted Happenings carry out risk-assessments for every location and take great care to inform guests of the potential hazards they may encounter, and in all my years nobody has ever been hurt.

However, it was that decision to move places at that moment which prevented a potential accident that night.

In addition to The Rack there was another piece of equipment around which our group had formed the circle, consisting of a rectangular base, upon which two vertical frames were positioned.

One merely had a carved-out semi-circle, over which the victim's arched back would rest, and the other contained two holes – through which their feet would be locked into place – resembling the stocks through which people's heads and hands are often placed at village fetes.

Its victims were positioned into the equipment and water pumped into their stomach, until such time as it could take no more and would rupture, causing certain and agonising death.

We had spent quite some time in this room already, moving into position and conducting our vigil, yet at no point had there been any indication either of these uprights were loose, or even that they *could* be moved.

However, literally seconds after one lady had stepped from within the framework of the base, there was a deafening crash.

Screams and confusion filled the room in an instant.

'Stand still,' I shouted at the top of my voice, desperate to be heard above the commotion and prevent anybody hurting themselves in the darkened room. 'Turn on your torches and stand still.'

As the room began to illuminate with the reassuring glow of torchlight, the source of the noise became apparent.

One of the vertical pieces had come crashing down and was now resting against the base-frame, exactly where the lady had been standing merely seconds earlier.

Horror consumed me as the realisation of how close this encounter had been dawned upon me, and the potential damage it could have caused.

People's faces dropped; genuine fear and confusion etched across them – mine included.

'Did any of us touch the frame when we moved?' I asked, convinced we must have caused this in some way. 'It's not a problem if we did,' I added, 'I just need to know if *we* caused that to happen.'

I chose my words carefully, using 'we' and 'us' instead of 'you', to avoid anybody feeling accused.

Everyone said no and the lady who had been closest to it confirmed she had stepped in the opposite direction, and had been the last to move.

With people beginning to calm a little I stepped forward to re-position the frame, and was astounded by what I discovered.

My scepticism wouldn't allow me to believe this wasn't an accident and that, inadvertently, somebody had brushed against the frame causing it to fall; they were probably just too embarrassed to say.

However, when I tried to lift the wood back into place, the sheer weight of it took me by surprise. I had to bend my knees and use all of my strength just to lift it.

Reluctant to cause any damage, I chose not to recreate the incident, but once back in place we applied pressure to the upright and concluded it would have taken a deliberate push – with some force and determination – to make it fall in the way it had.

With the combination of the cranking noise we had heard from The Rack and the near-miss we had just encountered, we were thankful it was time to re-group with the others and end the night.

Bran Castle had most certainly given us all something to think about!

But it wasn't over yet!

The Tunnels

Deep in the bowels of the hillside, beneath the castle itself, there is a secret tunnel.

The tunnel links the castle's interior courtyard with the Royal Park, and was used by Queen Mary when she wanted to gain access to the park without having to walk down the steep slope from the fortress.

Accessed via a heavy wooden door, the tunnel is around forty meters in length. The dusty floor is comprised of sub-soil and gravel, and the walls – with arched ceiling above – are made of crumbling stone.

Inside, in the dead of night, the blackness is all-consuming, and when everyone is silent the feeling of utter isolation is overwhelming.

This was to be our final vigil before leaving the castle, and the whole group – some twenty-two people – positioned themselves along the tunnel, spaced apart at intervals of a few feet.

With only the soft glow of one or two K2 meters to offer respite from the darkness, the vigil had begun with little effect.

One or two people in the group had reported hearing strange noises, and after someone threw a small piece of gravel, others said they believed they'd heard it thrown back.

Two people had already left the space after feeling so uncomfortable that they couldn't continue.

Little did I realise that I was about to join them.

In all the years I have been involved with paranormal investigations I have never experienced anything physical or actually sensed anything unexplained myself.

That doesn't mean I'm less inclined to believe when others report these sensations, but because I'd never experienced anything similar I always found it difficult to relate to what they felt in their moment of fear.

But that was about to change.

While standing in the darkness, surrounded by other ghost hunters and listening to their voices calling out for someone to make themselves known, I began to drift.

I can only liken it to the way television shows portray a scene where a person is drifting in and out of consciousness. I was aware of those around me and could hear their voices, yet I didn't feel part of the room. I felt distant, as though I couldn't reach out to them. It was as though I wasn't really there anymore.

Then the vision came.

Feeling somewhat uneasy, I had made the decision to close my eyes, just in case my brain was causing these feelings while trying to make sense of the darkness and surroundings. But, moments after I closed them, three faces rushed up towards me.

Three grey, wispy faces; one after another and in quick succession.

I cannot describe it in any other way than to liken them to the Dementors in J.K Rowling's *Harry Potter*.

Faces without structure. A mouth, but not a mouth. Perceptible dents where the eyes should be, but no eyes. And with these faces, the most horrible feeling I have ever encountered. Absolute dread and emptiness.

I left the tunnel and didn't return!

I cannot explain what happened down there. Having conducted ghost hunts in places equally as daunting as the tunnels, I felt sure I'd not allowed my imagination run away with me.

I began to question if I was simply so tired that I had hallucinated, or even somehow fallen asleep while standing. I tried every way to find a rational answer for what had just happened, and I couldn't. In fact, I never have.

I know I was awake because I could hear everything around me. I know it wasn't my eyes playing tricks on me in the dark because not only am I used to conducting vigils in similar conditions, but my eyes were closed.

Had it just been the images which flew into my head I'd have put it down to tiredness, but those feelings – the hollow emptiness and nausea I felt – were real.

I believe that, in the bowels of those tunnels beneath Bran Castle, I encountered something very unpleasant; something I never wish to experience ever again.

~ The End ~

A NOTE FROM THE AUTHOR

This book has been a long time in the making, but after almost ten years of ghost hunting – and an array of bizarre experiences in a number of 'haunted' locations – I felt it was time to share those stories.

The events are portrayed here to the best of my memory. While the stories and conversations in this book are based on actual experiences, some identifying details have been changed or omitted to protect the privacy and anonymity of the people involved.

This collection of stories are written from my own perspective and do not necessarily constitute fact, nor are they a reflection of Haunted Happenings' views or opinions.

I've had an incredible time working with Haunted Happenings since 2009, and hope you've enjoyed reading about those experiences just as much as I've enjoyed writing about them.

Thank you for reading my book.

If you enjoyed your read it would be massively appreciated if you would hop over to Amazon and leave a review. If you didn't enjoy it then there's no rush ☺

Please feel free to loan it to friends and family, and rather than leaving it to gather dust on a bookshelf, why not consider donating it to a charity shop?

To book an overnight ghost hunting experience with Haunted Happenings visit www.hauntedhappenings.co.uk

 @hauntedhappeningsuk   @hauntedhapp

Printed in Great Britain
by Amazon